RESTRAINT and SECLUSION

The Model for Eliminating Their Use in Healthcare

Tim Murphy, MS
Maggie Bennington-Davis, MD

Foreword by Sandra L. Bloom, MD

hcPro

Restraint and Seclusion: The Model for Eliminating Their Use in Healthcare is published by HCPro, Inc.

Copyright 2005 by HCPro, Inc.

All rights reserved. Printed in the United States of America.   5 4 3 2 1

ISBN 1-57839-622-0

Except where specifically encouraged, no part of this publication may be reproduced, in any form or by any means, without prior written consent of HCPro, Inc. or the Copyright Clearance Center (978/750-8400). Please notify us immediately if you have received an unauthorized copy. Arrangements can be made for quantity discounts.

HCPro, Inc., provides information resources for the healthcare industry. HCPro, Inc., is not affiliated in any way with the Joint Commission on Accreditation of Healthcare Organizations, which owns the JCAHO trademark. The JCAHO continues to make changes to its survey process and standards. The information in this book is current as of publication. If the JCAHO makes significant changes, HCPro will publish them in **Briefings on JCAHO** or on *www.hcpro.com*.

Tim Murphy, MS, Author
Maggie Bennington-Davis, MD, Author
Amy Anthony, Managing Editor
David Cella, Executive Editor
Matthew Cann, Group Publisher
Suzanne Perney, Publisher
Jean St. Pierre, Creative Director
Jackie Diehl Singer, Graphic Artist
Laura Godinho, Cover Designer
Lauren Rubenzahl, Copy Editor
Paul Singer, Layout Artist

Advice given is general. Readers should consult professional counsel for specific legal, ethical, or clinical questions. For more information on this or other HCPro, Inc., publications, contact:

HCPro, Inc.
P.O. Box 1168
Marblehead, MA 01945
Telephone: 800/650-6787 or 781/639-1872
Fax: 800/639-8511 or 781/639-2982
E-mail: *customerservice@hcpro.com*

Visit HCPro, Inc., at our World Wide Web sites:
www.hcmarketplace.com and *www.hcpro.com*

Contents

About the authors v
Acknowledgements vii
Foreword viii
Introduction xi

Chapter 1: Developing the vision 1
    The call for reform 3
    Transforming the system 4
    Obstacles to the vision 5
    Being the visionary 6

Chapter 2: Trauma-informed care 7
    What is trauma-informed care? 9
    The trauma-informed environment 10
    Trauma-informed treatment 13
    Value of a trauma-informed system 13

Chapter 3: Preparing the organization for change 15
    Steps to changing a culture 17
    Becoming data-driven 22
    Survey for 'change-readiness' 23

Chapter 4: Building the management team and developing the leadership process 27
    Assess your current management team 29
    Use focused retreats 30
    Create the motivation to change 31
    Restraint and seclusion initiative 32

Chapter 5: Components of cultural change 37
    Leveling the hierarchy 39
    Power and control 39
    Language and vocabulary 41
    Attitude adjustment: Serving our guests 43
    Changing expectations and beliefs 44

Contents

    Learning communities, rituals, and traditions 45
    Creating new assumptions: Hope and recovery 46

Chapter 6: Implementation 49
    Physical environment 51
    Social environment 53
    Community meeting 54
    Staff-to-staff interactions 56
    Staff-to-patient interactions 57
    Admission process 57
    Risk assessment 58
    Safety 58

Chapter 7: Restraint and seclusion events: Debriefing a big deal 61
    Debriefing goals 64

Chapter 8: Supporting the plan 75
    Culture bearers at all times 77
    Selecting new employees 78
    Orienting and training new employees 79
    Incorporating physicians 80

Chapter 9: Accreditation 83
    JCAHO standards 85
    JCAHO Everyday 87

Chapter 10: Lessons learned 91
    Lesson one: Identify your partners 93
    Lesson two: Gain leadership buy-in 94
    Lesson three: Involve the payers 96
    Lesson four: Predict uncertainty 96
    Lesson five: Take advantage of collateral benefits 97

Chapter 11: Summary 101

Appendix: The Engagement Model: A quick reference guide 103
    Introduction 105
    Components of change 106
    Intensive analysis of seclusion and restraint 107
    Sample non-violence statement 108

Bibliography 115

About the authors

Tim Murphy, MS

Tim Murphy, MS, is the chief executive officer of Evolutions in Healthcare, a consulting firm for hospitals and healthcare systems committed to quality improvement using evidence-based practices.

Murphy has more than 20 years of experience in both the public and private mental health fields. Murphy is a family therapist by training and a hospital administrator for more than seven years by practice. His background includes teaching, training, and start-ups, and he is a turnaround specialist for struggling psychiatric programs. Murphy recently represented Oregon's Association of Hospitals and Health Systems on the State of Oregon's Mental Health Task Force by appointment of the governor. The group is charged with rebuilding the mental health system in Oregon. He is also a member of the training faculty of the National Technical Assistance Center. He can be reached at *tim@evolutionsinhealthcare.com*.

Maggie Bennington-Davis, MD

Equipped with extensive physician leadership and clinical development experience in various roles, Maggie Bennington-Davis, MD, is cofounder of Evolutions in Healthcare and has served as medical director for psychiatry at Salem (OR) Hospital.

She is board certified in psychiatry and trained at Oregon Health Sciences University. While filling the role of Medical Director for Salem Hospital Psychiatry, Bennington-Davis (along with Murphy) developed a cultural-change model that eliminated the use of seclusion and restraint. She has facilitated workshops and training programs throughout the country and has assisted many organizations in implementing the model.

Bennington-Davis recently served as the medical staff president at Salem Hospital, a 400-bed hospital. She is particularly experienced in managing relationships among boards, medical staff, and management; peer review and performance improvement; physician leadership development; and cultural development. She participates on many system advisory boards for the public mental health system in Oregon and is a liaison between the American Hospital Association and the Joint Commission on Accreditation of Healthcare Organizations (JCAHO).

About the authors

Continuing her education in leadership, Bennington-Davis recently completed a master's degree in medical management at New Orleans–based Tulane University School of Public Health and Tropical Medicine.

In addition to her vast professional and academic duties, Bennington-Davis is a member of the American Psychiatric Association and the American College of Physician Executives. She also remains active at her alma mater, Oregon Health Sciences University, as a clinical teacher. Her recent awards include Oregon's 2003 State Award for Excellence in Mental Health Services and Salem Hospital's 2004 Leadership Excellence Award. This year she is the recipient of the American Association of Community Psychiatry's 2005 Ethics Award.

Acknowledgements

We wish to acknowledge, with sincere gratitude, Dr. Sandra Bloom for her teaching, coaching, mentoring, and friendship over the past several years. When the going got tough, Sandy kept us going. We honor and love her.

We would also like to recognize the staff and physicians of the Department of Psychiatry at Salem Hospital for their willingness and courage to put into practice what we imagined in theory.

However, it is the people we have served and their families that were our best teachers and to whom we dedicate this book. It was their wisdom that guided us and will continue to guide us in our never-ending effort to improve the provision of care for those with symptoms of mental illnesses.

Foreword

When Maggie Bennington-Davis and Tim Murphy first asked me to visit the psychiatric unit they had just started to manage, I wasn't sure what to expect. Although I had spent most of my life working in inpatient psychiatric units in urban settings, for the previous 10 years I had been running a specialty program for adult trauma survivors in the then well-financed private sector.[1] The first item on their agenda was to give me a tour of the place—as a prospective patient. In this role, I asked myself, "Would I want to be treated in this place? Would I want someone I loved to be admitted here?" And I began my tour. After climbing up a flight of stairs and walking into an open, reasonably inviting space, however, my eyes lit upon a prominently displayed sign at the unprepossessing and locked entrance to the unit: it read, "POLICE: LEAVE YOUR GUNS HERE."

Although surely not meant to mimic Dante's inscription written above the door to hell— "Abandon Hope All Ye Who Enter"—it had a similarly chilling effect. Within seconds, as an incoming patient, I had already learned that this was not likely to be a safe and healing refuge from a world that had overwhelmed me. This forbidding (albeit perfectly reasonable) instruction alerted me immediately to be on my guard, to expect violence, and to protect myself. It told me that this was a dangerous place.

As the tour continued, I was led into a small entry that housed the desk where I, as a patient, would answer admission questions and have my belongings and my person thoroughly searched. Here I would give up my own clothing and, like a prisoner, trade in my personal apparel—and a distinctive sense of my own identity—for an impersonal scrub suit. This alcove space, sealed off from the rest of the unit by a door, also housed the unit's several seclusion rooms so that hallucinatory murmurings, demands for attention, and loud demands for release provided an auditory accompaniment to my growing anxiety in my role as patient.

The unit itself was bright and spacious, was relatively quiet, and had little decoration or apparent activity because most of the patients were in their rooms and in bed. The staff were solicitous, but there were relatively few planned therapeutic activities, and the patients clearly believed that their daily visits with their psychiatrist and their medication regulation were their reasons for being there. There was a sense of order, but I gained few impressions of the real life of the place. More like a highly regulated and orderly hotel than like a place of healing, there was little sense of community, with individual members striving toward a shared goal of social learning.

At Maggie and Tim's direction, I began to meet with the staff and to talk with them about democratic therapeutic communities, community meetings, patient participation, trauma-informed psychoeducational groups, and what it takes to create a place of sanctuary that encourages and supports healing. At first the staff humored me and listened politely, but later they became emboldened to tell me, "That sounds wonderful, but it can't happen here—not with our patients."

In these early training sessions, we talked a great deal about the issue of trauma because it is a profound problem that lurks behind most psychiatric and social dysfunction that results in hospitalization. Indeed, recent studies show that traumatic victimization and posttraumatic stress disorder are highly prevalent (51%–98% and 42% respectively) among persons with severe mental illness who are within public-sector mental health.[2, 3] In a review of a number of studies on physical and sexual assault against women with serious mental illness, the authors reported that across studies, between 51% and 97% of participants experienced lifetime physical or sexual assault, and a significant proportion of these had experienced multiple acts of victimization.[4] In one study of involuntary psychiatric patients, the rate of nonviolent criminal victimization was similar to that in the general population, but the rate of violent criminal victimization was two and a half times greater than in the general population.[5] And according to the Adverse Childhood Experiences Study, one in four middle-class white adults has been exposed to two categories of childhood adversity, and one in sixteen to at least four categories—and the more categories of adversity a person experiences, the more likely they are to suffer from a variety of physical and emotional disorders, including chronic depression, suicide attempts, and substance abuse.[6] Additional research also demonstrates that patients admitted to psychiatric facilities often describe experiences within these settings as traumatic, especially the use of coercive measures like restraint and seclusion. In one important study, 44% of patients said they had experienced physical or sexual assault while in a hospital, 39% had experienced coercive measures, 26% had witnessed physical violence, and 23% had experienced verbal abuse.[7]

In this guidebook, psychiatrist Bennington-Davis and hospital administrator Murphy describe how they finally convinced their staff that it could be done "here" with "our patients," and they share the lessons they learned along the way. Within a relatively short time, the psychiatrists, the management team, and the staff had indeed turned their program into an entirely different place, without increasing staff—in fact, this change happened during a period of staff cutbacks. They reduced the use of restraint and seclusion to a point nearing total elimination. They reduced the use of emergency medications. They radically reduced the amount of violence on the unit and thereby reduced staff injuries, reduced workmen's compensation cases, and improved staff morale. And the unit became more fiscally sound than it had ever been.

In order to achieve these goals, they learned how to successfully engage patients in shared goal-setting, co-creation of safe community, and collaborative treatment planning. With this book, they hope to convince others that changing an environment from one of coercion and abusive power to one of Sanctuary is not only morally necessary and fiscally responsible but also fundamentally possible for any program whose staff is committed to positive change.

Sandra L. Bloom, MD
Distinguished Fellow, Sanctuary Leadership Development Institute
Andrus Children's Center, Yonkers, NY

Foreword

1. S.L. Bloom, *Creating Sanctuary: Toward the Evolution of Sane Societies*. (New York: Routledge, 1997).
2. G.E. Switzer, et al., "Posttraumatic stress disorder and service utilization among urban mental health center clients," *Journal of Traumatic Stress*, 1999. 12: pp. 25–39.
3. K. Mueser, et al., "Trauma and posttraumatic stress disorder in severe mental illness," *Journal of Consulting and Clinical Psychology*, 1998. 66: pp. 493–499.
4. L.A. Goodman, et al., "Physical and sexual assault history in women with serious mental illness: prevalence, correlates, treatment, and future research directions," *Schizophrenia Bulletin*, 1997. 23(4): pp. 685–96.
5. V.A. Hiday, et al., "Criminal victimization of persons with severe mental illness," *Psychiatric Services*, 1999. 50(1): pp. 62–68.
6. V.J. Felitti, et al., "Relationship of childhood abuse and household dysfunction to many of the leading causes of death in adults: The Adverse Childhood Experiences (ACE) Study," *American Journal of Preventive Medicine*, 1998. 14(4): pp. 245–58.
7. K.J. Cusack, et al., "Trauma within the psychiatric setting: A preliminary empirical report," *Administration and Policy in Mental Health*, 2003. 30(5).

Introduction

The use of restraint and seclusion in healthcare settings—whether hospitals, psychiatric facilities, residential programs, or schools—has become such an integral part of the daily regimen that the title of this book may seem ludicrous at first glance.

Restraint use is commonplace in emergency rooms, intensive care units, cardiac care units, and stroke recovery units in most hospitals in the United States. Psychiatric facilities for children, adolescents, and adults have incorporated the use of restraint and seclusion so effectively that it is often thought of as a treatment.

This book is meant to dispel that notion and to help the reader understand the problems inherent in the use of restraint and seclusion—namely the relationship dynamic between the *treating professional* and the *treated patient*. When positive, this dynamic can foster improved understanding, improved environment of care, improved outcomes, and less chance of treatment failure.

We will introduce to you a model of care we have named the Engagement Model. It was developed over a period of four years as we co-led an acute care hospital's inpatient department of psychiatry, which included both inpatient and outpatient programs. This model redefines the relationship between the *treater* and the *treated* in order to minimize conflict and maximize collaboration and cooperation.

The healthcare industry is going through a revolution in almost all of its facets. New technology is leading to new treatments and improved care. The Internet has led to a far more educated patient who is demanding to be a "partner" in his or her own care. Medications appear to be changing every month or two, and the financial structures that fund our healthcare are being rebuilt right before our eyes. In short, nothing is constant. All parts of the system are improving and evolving. Those who cannot abide change have no place in the healthcare industry—now or in the future. Our approach toward restraint and seclusion must change with the times.

Although our specialty is psychiatric care, the issues that we discuss and the strategies that we recommend are not exclusive to mental health. They have much wider applications in healthcare and in other social systems where people congregate to work toward common goals. We have taken our ideas to schools, residential communities, and correctional organizations and have been met with interest and excitement.

Introduction

This book is laid out in a linear fashion. We start with the realization that to bring about change in a work culture, where people interact in a variety of roles, there must first be a clear vision about and strong recognition of the need to create change in order to meet the higher goal of an improved outcome. We discuss building the vision, delivering the message, assessing the organization's readiness and needs for change, and organizing the leadership needed to move the initiative forward.

We give you concrete examples of how to implement a change process and what to expect along the way. We have included examples of things that may (and will) go wrong and how to address them, correct them, and continue to move forward.

We share with you our journey from more than 365 seclusions in a year to one seclusion in the past two years, and from hundreds of episodes of leather or mechanical restraint use to zero in nearly three years. We are proof positive that you can reduce coercive measures and improve treatment outcomes.

We hope you will be excited, stimulated, challenged, and motivated by what you read here, and we encourage you to begin today to create the environment you want for yourselves, your patients, your residents, and your students.

Tim Murphy, MS
Maggie Bennington-Davis, MD

Developing the vision

CHAPTER 1

Developing the vision

Healing is always possible, even when curing is not.
—Brigit of Ireland

Something has gone awry in the system we use to treat severe mental illness. An article in the *New England Journal of Medicine* read, "The pharmacologic treatment of mental illness has become so successful that psychiatry no longer needs to focus on the psyche." In its zeal to cure people of their symptoms, the delivery system we use has been distorted to the point that it alienates the very people we seek to serve. We must do better.

Successful efforts exist to decrease and even eliminate use of restraint and seclusion in hospitals. But why *should* restraint and seclusion be eliminated?

The call for reform

The simplest reason for reform is that physical and mechanical restraint is dangerous to patients and staff and has caused significant injuries and deaths to those restrained. Reform has been demanded by the Centers for Medicare & Medicaid Services, the Joint Commission on Accreditation of Healthcare Organizations, the National Association of State Mental Health Program Directors, and the National Alliance for the Mentally Ill, as well as numerous consumers groups and the American Psychiatric Association.

In addition to the dangers associated with them, restraint and seclusion are problematic because they frequently are used as punishment and coercion. They are applied inconsistently and subjectively in many facilities. They are not therapeutic interventions; in fact, they traumatize both those who experience them and those who administer them. The experience of restraint and seclusion causes alienation from the mental health system, from treatment staff, and from physicians. It disrupts potentially therapeutic relationships and interferes with engagement in treatment. The use of these interventions perpetuates the cycles of violence and trauma that many of the people we serve already have experienced.

Chapter 1

Transforming the system

In addition to the aforementioned healthcare agencies calling for reform, the Institute of Medicine outlined the following improvement in 2001 (National Executive Training Institute):
- Continuous, healing relationships
- Customization of treatment to individual needs and values
- Consumer/patient control of treatment
- Risk reduction to ensure safety
- Transparent information about healthcare practices and systems

In 2003, President Bush's New Freedom Commission called for system transformation in which
- recovery is a goal for everyone
- services are consumer-centered
- focus of care increases consumers' ability to self-manage illness and to build resiliency
- consumers and families are full partners in patient recovery

Those that have already successfully decreased and eliminated use of restraint and seclusion have demonstrated that sustained improvement requires a fundamental shift in thinking about the people they serve, their illnesses and symptoms, and the staff who serve them. Indeed, the practices of restraint and seclusion are significantly tied to other coercive practices, and cultural change is required in order to intercede (National Executive Training Institute).

In order to change basic beliefs and assumptions about people with symptoms of mental illness and about the illnesses themselves, mental health systems and the care they deliver must become trauma-informed. Staff must change their fundamental approach to the treatment environment from one of power and control to one of customer service. Both staff and the people they serve must experience their relationships in new ways—with respect, hope, dignity, and involvement.

This magnitude of organizational change and the organizational dynamics that are involved in it requires leadership. The first task of such leadership is to imagine a new version of the future: a future in which healers create an environment of engagement and healing and where miracles can happen.

Obstacles to the vision

The main obstacle to cultural change is old paradigms: "We've always done it that way before." "It has worked for 20 years." "This is what I was taught in school."

Organizations that have undergone successful transformational change share two key features: leadership and vision. Leaders establish direction through a vision, and a compelling vision is the first step to shifting the paradigm. The vision guides decisions, performance, culture, and attitude. It motivates all members of the organization to work toward something better. Vision gives meaning to our work. It fixes a standard of excellence. It insists that all employees give their best. It energizes people and inspires them to a future to which they are eager to commit. A vision is not only helpful in the change that is required for this particular transformation in healthcare; it is essential.

A vision summarizes the ideal state of an organization. It can come from either influential and powerful leaders or from the collective voices of the organization. Where it comes from is less important than ensuring that it is driven by specific values that staff share, that they understand, and to which they commit.

To begin, imagine five years from now. Imagine the most desirable situation you can conceive, for you, for the people you serve, and for your staff. Describe what you imagine, as if it were a painting or a picture. Use words and drawings; use metaphors and images. Draw on beliefs and values. Weave in current realities and the environment of your work.

A new vision is fragile. Tradition, hierarchy, stereotypes, stigma, bigotry, complacency, and fear of ridicule are all enemies of vision. Change is overwhelming for many people and organizations, especially if people don't know where they are headed or why. Therefore, once conceived, communicate, share, and translate the vision so that everyone in the organization understands and connects to it. Adopting it will provide energy and direction to the mission.

Examples of vision

- To create an environment where the healed and the healers work together to find paths to recovery

- To eliminate the weapons of power, control, and coercion—including restraint and seclusion—so that the environment is optimized for partnership in healing

- To create a place of absolute safety and respect for the staff and the people we serve

Chapter 1

- To work together with those we serve in a trauma-informed, intelligent, and safe environment in which person-centered treatment is facilitated

- To work in an environment where restraint and seclusion are unnecessary and where the alternatives of respect, kindness, safety, and education replace them

Being the visionary

The purpose of this book is to lay out a pathway for those who serve the mentally ill, whether in a hospital, in a residential program, in an outpatient setting, or in a school. We must learn new ways to engage in the process of healing. These ways must depend on cooperation, collaboration, hope, and trust, which are the very things missing from today's treatment strategies for those suffering from mental illness.

New ideas and new strategies always emerge from the visionaries. Someone has to develop the vision that drives the plan that creates the change that improves the service.

In the Engagement Model, we call on a full-scale culture change where the treater and the treated forge a new alliance, with recovery as the goal and partnership and respect as the pathway. The vision does not have to strive for the elimination of restraint and seclusion (ours did not); instead it may call for an environment free from coercion. Or it may call for a new partnership between patients and treatment care staff in which the patients are involved in all decisions involving their care, such as meal times, visitors, lengths of stay, and how their specific treatment is to be delivered. With visions like these, the need for controlling mechanisms like seclusion, restraint, and time-outs—and the injuries associated with them—become relics of the past.

Once the vision is set, a leadership team must be identified. That leadership community will develop the plan to create the culture where the vision can be realized.

In Chapter 4, we look at how you build your leadership team using your current management structure and what you may need to to do in order to augment the leadership skills that already exist.

Key points in this chapter

1. Significant change must be leadership-driven
2. Leaders need to establish a clear vision for change
3. Engagement between the treated and those providing treatment is the goal of the change for reducing restraint and seclusion

Trauma-informed care

CHAPTER 2

Trauma-informed care

As many as 90% (Muesar, 1998) of people who require hospitalization because of symptoms of mental illness have coexisting—and, perhaps, precipitating—histories of trauma.

The National Association of State Mental Health Program Directors offered this definition of trauma in 2004: "The personal experience of interpersonal violence including sexual abuse, physical abuse, severe neglect, loss, and/or the witnessing of violence, terrorism and disasters." The 2000 American Psychiatric Association's definition of a traumatic event is one in which a person "experienced, witnessed or was confronted with an event(s) that involved actual or threatened death or serious injury or threat to the physical integrity of self or others."

Those we serve in hospitals frequently have histories of many such events in their lifetimes, aggravated by the trauma of police pick-up, physical restraint, isolation from others during the scariest moments of their lives, involuntary medication administration, involuntary hospitalization, and the experience of psychotic or severe mood symptoms.

What is trauma-informed care?

Trauma-informed care is mental health treatment that is directed with a thorough understanding of the profound neurological, biological, psychological, and social effects of trauma and violence on an individual and with an appreciation for the high incidence of traumatic experiences among people who receive mental health services (National Executive Training Institute, NASMHPD).

Although mental health providers are adept at recognizing post-traumatic stress disorder as a single, stand-alone entity, we are less likely to recognize that those with schizophrenia and bipolar disorder are also likely to manifest the neurobiological aftermath of traumatic experience.

Trauma leaves its mark throughout the developmental spectrum. Over the long term, it can change brain neurobiology; create social, emotional, and cognitive impairment;

Chapter 2

trigger adoption of health risk behaviors as coping mechanisms (e.g., substance abuse, self-harm, violence, smoking, eating disorders, sexual promiscuity); and lead to severe and persistent behavioral health, physical health, and social problems, as well as early death (Felitti et al., 1998). Traumatized children exhibit guarded and anxious affects, are highly emotionally reactive, have difficulty calming down after outbursts, hold onto grievances, do not take responsibility for behavior, and make the same mistakes over and over again (Hodas, 2004).

Acute reactions to trauma include hypervigilance, an increased startle reaction, loss of ability to communicate verbally, decreased impulse control, impaired cognition, and increased aggression (Bloom, 1996). When exposure to traumatic events is repeated and becomes chronic, the autonomic nervous system resets so that the person exhibits chronic hyperarousal that interferes with cognitive clarity; leads to chronic aggression, a tendency toward traumatic reenactment, and loss of affect modulation; and reinforces a sense of helplessness.

Keeping in mind that a majority of people we serve with severe psychiatric symptoms are thus described, what happens when they are secluded or restrained? They tell us that they experience shame, guilt, and humiliation. Their fear increases, and they have a sense of abandonment, helplessness, and vulnerability. They express feelings of fear, rejection, and anger. They feel punished and confused, and their bitterness and anger persist long after the event. (Wadeson et al., 1976; Martinez, 1999; Mann et al., 1993; Ray et al., 1996; Mohr, 1999; National Executive Training Institutes.)

Trauma-informed systems are structured to incorporate what we know about the incidence and neurobiology of trauma into the experience of mental health treatment—and they include the point of view of the people they serve. Above all, they recognize that coercion causes further trauma and alienation (Najavits, 2003). In fact, mental health treatment environments are often coercive and traumatizing—overtly and covertly—and a majority of mental health treatment staff remain uninformed about trauma, its incidence, and its sequelae and fail to recognize it or treat it (National Executive Training Institutes: Fallot and Harris, 2003; Cook et al., 2003; Jennings, 1998; Prescott, 2000).

The trauma-informed environment

There are several approaches to developing a trauma-informed environment, all of which begin with the education of staff, physicians, families, and the people we serve. The education includes the definition of trauma, the stories of those who have experienced it, an examination of its prevalence among those we serve, the identification of it, and the response to it within the treatment environment. Then the admission process incorporates this perspective by focusing on asking "what happened to you" instead of "what is wrong with you" (Bloom, 1994) and gathering a trauma history in the context of a trusting relationship.

Trauma-informed care

The trauma history addresses experiences of past or current trauma, violence, and abuse and specifically asks about trauma experienced in the context of treatment, such as restraint and seclusion, involuntary admission, and involuntary medication. This conversation is extremely important, as it provides both a context for the other symptoms the person may be experiencing and a glimpse into what the person may be expecting in your environment.

Note, however, as mentioned above, that traumatized individuals may not be able to readily trust mental health professionals, may be experiencing retraumatization simply by virtue of their current situation in your facility, and may not be able to verbalize in a way that provides the pertinent information. Therefore, always assume that people in your facility have been exposed to some form of abuse, coercion, and violence, and proceed on that assumption.

The treatment plan, therefore, is trauma-informed by being created and driven by the individual it serves, by being unique and individualized, by containing hope, and by assuming recovery. The environment shows evidence of trauma sensitivity by its culture of respect, service, safety, and participation.

Figure 2.1 — Trauma history questions, triggers, and coping strategies

Obtaining a trauma history

History of trauma and violence
Include trauma
- inflicted in hospitals
    - seclusion
    - restraint
    - forced medication
    - severe medication side effects
- of psychosis or severe mood or anxiety symptoms
- of police pick-up
- of institutionalization
- of stigmatization
- of being diagnosed with a serious mental illness

Include history of
- being assaulted
- assaulting another
- childhood physical, emotional, and sexual abuse
- abandonment
- traumatic loss

| Figure 2.1 | **Trauma history questions, triggers, and coping strategies (cont.)** |

Ask, "what happened to you?" (as opposed to, "What is wrong with you?")

Common triggers include
- enforcement of agency rules
- perception of unfair treatment
- waiting
- anger about past experience in the mental health system
- controlling, restrictive environment
- shame and humiliation
- fear
- crowding
- boredom
- physical discomfort

Examples of coping strategies
- walking
- music
- talking
- lying down
- time alone
- reading
- writing
- hot shower
- deep breathing
- calling support person
- bouncing a ball
- male staff
- female staff
- humor
- crying
- spiritual practice
- therapist
- being read to

Endnote: Carmen E., Crane W., Dunnicliff M., Holochuck S., Prescott L., Reiker P.P., Stephen S., Stromberg N., (1996). *Massachusetts Department of Mental Health task force on the Restraint and Seclusion of persons who have been physically or sexuallly abused: report and recommendations.* Boston, MA: Department of Mental Health.

Trauma-informed treatment

Trauma-informed treatment plans incorporate a plan for safety while the patient is in the treatment environment. These plans begin with identification, by the person served, of triggers of past traumatic events, anxiety, fear, and anger. A good therapist or nurse can brainstorm a list of such triggers and then give equal time to exploring what the most helpful coping strategies have been. An inexpensive and effective way to implement this part of the safety plan is to list the person's triggers on one side of a piece of paper, list coping strategies on the other, and laminate the paper into a wallet-sized card that can be carried and referred to throughout hospitalization.

Value of a trauma-informed system

Treatment environments that are coercive, disrespectful, and marked by power and control relationships indicate uninformed systems. In medicine, where we are taught to "first, do no harm," we face a moral imperative to eliminate seclusion and restraint as further traumatization of those we seek to serve.

The value of a trauma-informed system and of delivering trauma-informed care is that it decreases the conflict that is inherent in the treatment of the involuntary patient. Whenever conflict can be minimized, the opportunity for treatment increases. With increased opportunity for treatment, the road to recovery is less bumpy, and the length of the course of treatment (particularly inpatient) is reduced. Likewise, in nonhospital environments like residential care settings or schools, avoiding conflict by recognizing and responding in a trauma-informed way can also reduce conflict and increase the option of engagement.

Chapter 2

Figure 2.2 — **Sample triggers/strategies card**

The card is the size of a driver's license or credit card. Each facility has its own content in the two areas from which to choose. The following is one example:

Side A

Triggers for anxiety and distress

1. Feeling scared
2. Feeling trapped
3. Feeling crowded
4. Visits with brother
5. Being ignored

Side B

Coping strategies

1. Instant calming sequence
2. Listening to music
3. Talking to a peer
4. Being assertive
5. Communicating in writing

Key points in this chapter

1. Trauma-informed care is mental health treatment that is directed by a thorough understanding of the profound neurological, biological, psychological, and social effects of trauma and violence on an individual
2. Trauma-informed systems recognize the importance and value of trauma-informed care and incorporate that value in all phases of its work
3. Trauma-informed systems require trauma-informed treatment

Preparing the organization for change

CHAPTER 3

Preparing the organization for change

If we want to create a workplace that values idealism, human connection, and real, in-depth learning, we will have to create it ourselves.
–Peter Block

A few years ago, during a staff meeting in which we were discussing change, a nurse on the inpatient unit sighed.

"We're tired of change," the nurse said. "Can't we just stop where we are for a while?"

As a popular bumper sticker reads: Change happens.

You might be in an organization that is used to change and good at it, but chances are better (at least in healthcare organizations) that major cultural changes are met with resistance and, if done poorly, are doomed to disappointment. The particular change of moving away from coercion—including restraint and seclusion—toward a trauma-informed, customer-service, patient-centered approach to inpatient mental health treatment challenges the following basic notions that many of us in mental health are trained to believe:
- Patients want to be controlled
- Seclusion is therapeutic
- Restraint is necessary for safety
- Trained staff know better than patients what is best for them

This chapter provides a basic framework for how to think about and execute change in any healthcare environment.

Steps to changing a culture

Just as the patient milieu is a social community in which people take their cues from each other and behave accordingly, a hospital is a social system that strongly influences employees and physicians through its culture. Just as the most effective way to eliminate violence on the inpatient unit is to change culture, the most effective tool for organizational improvement is cultural change.

A hospital's culture—its shared beliefs, values, language, and customs—affect the way people work. Changing the culture is accomplished most effectively by using a planned approach to remove obstacles, increase motivation, and align changes with employees' values and rewards. Cultures can be influenced to change through work with overt behaviors, language, work processes, and social systems.

Step one: Decide who should be 'on the bus'

An essential first step to implementing the nonviolent model we describe in this book is to guide the organization out of its rigid, hierarchical structure and culture. Doing so helps develop a democratic decision-making process, a creative and flexible set of therapeutic responses that our complex patients require, and the leadership necessary to support these changes so that the system does not deteriorate into chaos.

In his book *Good to Great*, Jim Collins modifies the conventional wisdom from "people are your most important asset" to "the RIGHT people are your most important asset" in your organization. Indeed, the process of change begins well before the visible change, and as the vision takes shape, you must consider who the right people are to populate the new culture.

Jim Collins asks, "Who should be on the bus" that is traveling toward the vision? Once the right people are identified, ask them if they are sitting in the right seats. Act before the change begins if it is time for some people to "leave the bus." Then, the once the right people are in the right seats and the wrong people have departed, ensure participation by everyone on the trip.

Watch for early adopters of the new vision. In most organizations, 5%–15% of people will immediately endorse change. These people are the heralds and champions of positive change and your change efforts.

A word about physicians

Many organizations fail to include or involve physicians in major change initiatives, but that is a mistake—physicians can help the change initiative succeed or can sabotage it completely.

In eliminating restraint and seclusion, it is not only helpful but imperative that physicians be involved in and integrated into the change process from the beginning. Like many other professionals, they are often resistant to the idea of change—any change. But when added to the planning group, physicians are more likely to understand the need to change and share the vision. They will be extremely valuable in helping to develop both the data and measurement tools and ideas about how to reach the vision. They also are driven toward excellence, respond to information and data, and can be excellent problem-solvers. There are other reasons that they are better to have on the team than fighting it. Specifically, physicians have considerable influence on staff and the people they serve. They are often seen as leaders in their healthcare settings by families, patients, and staff. Their behavior, language, and beliefs flavor organizational culture and act as models for staff. If they think change is a good idea—or a bad idea—others are likely to follow suit.

Step two: Assess change readiness

Preparing your organization for a shift will begin with your vision and the leadership team, identification of your culture-bearers (old and new), and a roadmap for where you want to be. The Stages of Change model (Prochaska, DiClemente, 1983) uses precontemplative, contemplative, preparation, action, and maintenance stages to describe readiness for change.

Precontemplative stage

The precontemplative stage is characterized by the absence of even considering the need for change. An organization may be in this stage due to the subconscious belief that the risks of change would outweigh the benefits, due to the absence of information that leads one to consider change, or due to the experience of having tried but failed to change in the past, which creates feelings of helplessness and hopelessness about real change as an option. If one's organization is at this stage, raising consciousness about the need and opportunity for change is the main task.

Contemplative stage

The contemplative stage is characterized by the presence of the idea of change, often accompanied by feelings of ambivalence. There is a risk of becoming stuck in this stage and of gaining a reputation for being all talk and no action. The main task of the leaders at this stage is to provide staff with a concrete roadmap and a how-to promise for action.

Preparation stage

The preparation stage used to be called the decision-making stage. It is the transition from thought to action—decisions are made, and firm plans are put in place for moving forward. It is especially important at this time to recognize and celebrate short-term goals and early wins.

It is also the time for intensive education and support. In this stage, the organization must provide resources for specific training and education. External educators and mentors can be extremely valuable, as it is truly difficult to be a prophet in one's own land. Experts and mentors from outside the organization can lend leaders credibility with staff, provide external validation for the vision and ideas, and support leaders. External educators also level the hierarchy when leaders are seen by staff as learning at their side, puzzling over challenges with the rest of staff, and problem-solving in real time with their physicians.

Action stage

In the action stage, there is overt behavioral change. New coping strategies develop and replace old behaviors. Unexpectedly, there is often grief and loss associated with this forward progress, as old ways become obsolete.

The tasks of this stage are to support the new strategies, openly acknowledge and discuss the loss of the old culture, and recognize the temptation to revert to old ways during the most stressful times. Staff need to know what to do *instead* of what they've been doing. This is a moment to clarify the vision, revisit the concept of cultural change, and tell staff what specific behaviors to use in particular situations.

Maintenance stage
In the maintenance stage, the new behaviors have been maintained over time and begin to blend into a new culture. They no longer feel new but have become established responses to even the most stressful situations. The experience of successes with the new approaches has, in and of itself, become reinforcement and is part of the fabric of daily work. At this stage, the task is to ensure that all systems and cultural components are in sync with the new strategies. The development of internal trainers and educators helps anchor the organization's new culture.

A word about the stages
Throughout all of the change stages, there is the likelihood and risk of relapse. Any stage can revert to any former stage. This is a normal part of change. The leaders' task during relapse is to avoid overreaction and maybe even to predict relapse and to recognize that it is likely a temporary condition.

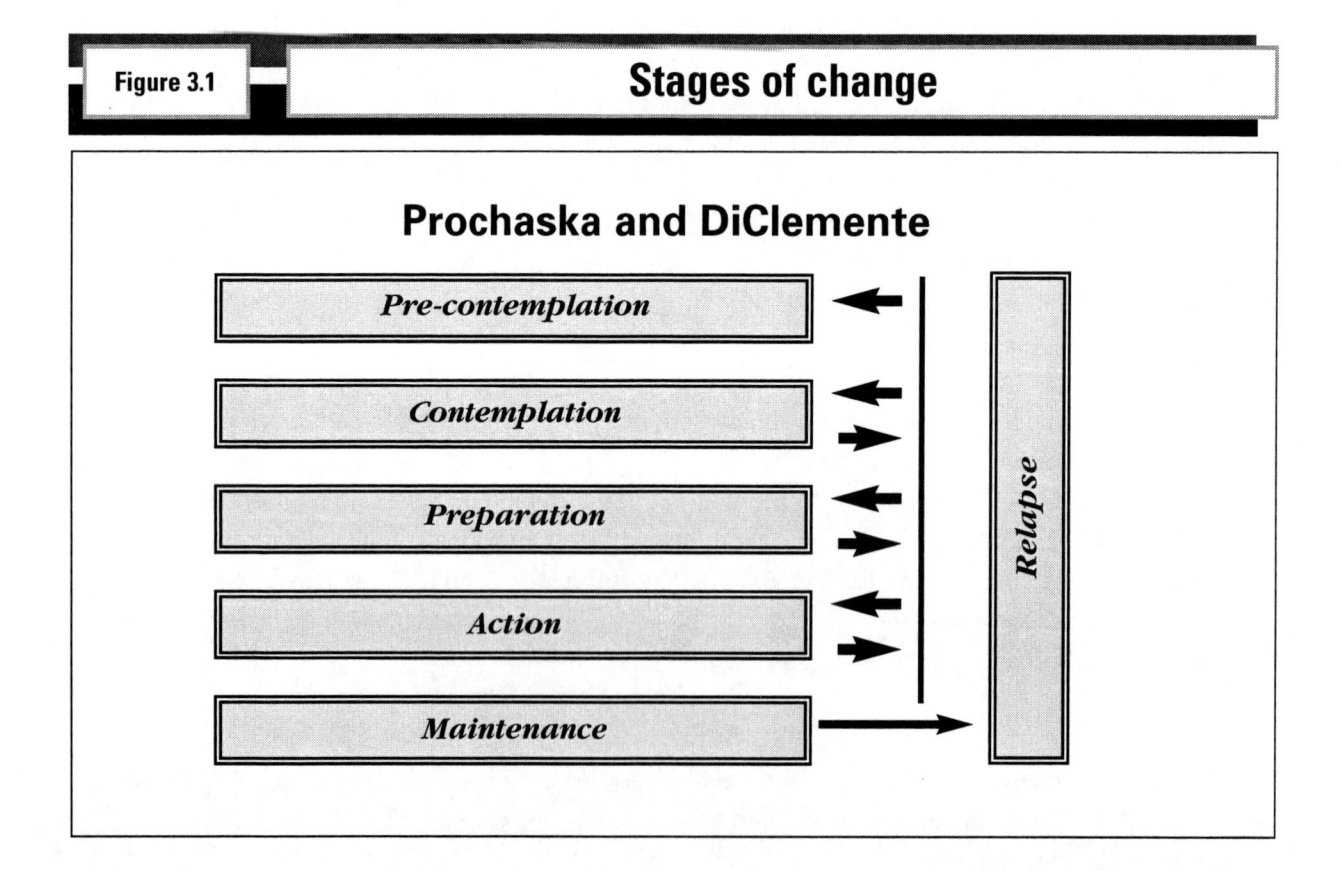

Figure 3.1 — Stages of change

Prochaska and DiClemente

- *Pre-contemplation*
- *Contemplation*
- *Preparation*
- *Action*
- *Maintenance*

Relapse

Preparing the organization for change

In his book *Managing Transitions*, William Bridges, describes a process of Letting Go (but keeping some) of the old ways (using the idea that transition begins with an ending), entering a Neutral Zone in which the old ways are no longer applicable but the new are not yet concretized (a time of chaos and creativity), and, finally, the New Beginning, when the new ways are in place (the idea that transition ends with a beginning).

Bridges recommends that leaders not be surprised when Letting Go draws an "over" reaction and the idea that suggests that they acknowledge loss and be open and sympathetic to the staff's response. Staff are hungry for information during the preparation for change, and it is important to give it to them over and over and over again. Describe the coming changes specifically and repeatedly. Map out openly what changes affect whom and how.

He also reminds leaders to treat the past respectfully. Staff members are often defensive when change begins because they believe that the new ways represent personal failures of the old ways.

Bridges outlines several useful do's and don'ts, which we summarize below:

Always
- be aware of who must change
- be aware of who will be affected
- market the vision aggressively
- talk to individuals and groups
- describe the process of transition; predict reactions
- listen intently and obviously; seek input

As much as you're able
- align new behaviors with rewards
- design stop-gaps between new and old
- make your mentors visible to staff
- change incentives to reward teamwork

Sometimes
- rearrange which staff work with which staff
- reorganize your management team
- include outside partners
- appeal to a higher authority

Avoid
- turning the project over to the individual contributors as a group and asking them to come up with a plan
- shrinking the vision and separating the components from the vision

Chapter 3

- giving up and finding a less disruptive plan
- becoming a disciplinarian regarding the change

Whatever change model you use, the success of your change ultimately depends on the people in your hospital *doing things differently*. You know you're making progress when restraint and seclusion don't even cross the minds of your staff members and of those they serve as they consider options for calming down a stressed and active patient.

Two years into our hospital's change process, our inpatient unit admitted a man who had been admitted before and had experienced seclusion and restraint. He did not want to be in the hospital and was declining treatment, including the medications that had helped his symptoms of paranoia and hallucinations in the past. When three nurses entered his room with his oral medication, he was prepared to fight them as he refused it. He thought they would next restrain him and use injectable medicine, so he assumed a defensive stance, ready to do what was necessary to protect himself.

The nurses, however, did not restrain him. Instead, they broke into a song in three-part harmony and continued to sing as the man stood amazed, then looked confused, and finally laughed. He listened for several more seconds and then held out his hand and said, "Please give me the medicine." These nurses were *not* professional singers. During the next medication time, the three nurses again entered his room, and without hesitation, the man said that if they would just not sing, he would readily take the medicine.

Perhaps that too was a form of coercion, but it was a creative, friendly, humorous attempt to engage someone who had been traumatized by his prior hospital experiences. When this interaction occurred, we knew that staff members were successfully *doing things differently* and even *thinking differently*.

Becoming data-driven

As you prepare and navigate a major improvement, such as eliminating restraint and seclusion, you must become a data-driven organization.

Charts, graphs, trends, rates, and analysis of what you do and how you do it are essential performance improvement tools. Providing constant feedback to your staff, the people you serve and their families, and your physicians is a key feature of eliminating restraint and seclusion (and practically any other performance improvement activity).

When becoming data-driven, first find your organization's baseline. Set goals that can be measured, measure them, and communicate what you've discovered. The goals should be updated

Activity measured	Goal
Number of restraints per week (or month)	1/week
Time in restraint (average, maximum)	1 hour, 4 hours
Number of seclusion events per week (or month)	3/week
Time in locked seclusion (average, maximum)	2 hours, 4 hours
Number of injuries	0
Number of workers' compensation claims	30% reduction
Number of complaints	30% reduction
Patient satisfaction scores	20% improvement
Employee satisfaction scores	20% improvement
Physician satisfaction scores	20% improvement
Staff and physician attendance at Community Meeting	80%
Adherence to reporting process	96%
Staff attendance when reporting/discussing data	80%

constantly, always urging staff toward the next level of improvement, in increments that can be achieved and celebrated. Above are examples of data to collect and turn into graphs, trends, and control charts. Post them everywhere, and discuss them constantly. Remember, what you measure is what you manage.

Survey for 'change-readiness'

Change-readiness survey tools explore whether you've created the urgent message that change is necessary, whether the vision as they understand it is a reasonable approach to the need, and whether staff have a sense of "what's in it for them" and whether it will harm them.

Readiness surveys often include an assessment of whether employees have adequate trust in leadership and whether they have been through other unsuccessful or successful changes that influence their buy-in. They also evaluate whether staff receive the resources (i.e., training) they need to accomplish the change. Such cultural assessments evaluate the level of blame that occurs in the organization—is the change process to be driven by fear or by excitement? Is there a pact, either explicit or implicit, that as staff members carry out the changes, leadership will support them?

Chapter 3

> **Are you ready?**
>
> - Is the vision clear, and are you able to communicate it clearly?
> - Is the vision compelling?
> - Is the vision aligned with the values of staff and physicians?
> - Have you made the case for the need for change?
> - Are the right people on board?
> - Have the wrong people left?
> - Have the physicians been included in the plan?
> - Is leadership speaking with a single voice?
> - Are the leaders equipped to manage a major change initiative?
> - Are the leaders trustworthy and trusted?
> - Are there resources available for education and support?
> - Is there an organizational culture of respect and openness?
> - Is there good communication throughout the organization?
> - Is there a good roadmap? That is, will people know what to do?
> - Is there support available for employees from human resources?
> - Does the timetable allow for the stages of change?
> - Are there data and information systems available for feedback and measurement of progress?
> - Has the organization's history of responses to and success with past change initiatives been accounted for?

In general, readiness surveys ask how the organization plans to measure the effectiveness of its changes and the progress in making them. Such surveys, when completed honestly and by a broad cross-section of affected individuals, are very helpful as you consider the starting point of your cultural change project. Clearly, some individuals are more ready for change than others, and some are more on-board with your vision than others, but you get a sense of your *organization's* readiness by considering these issues.

Once you determine that your organization is ready, begin communicating the vision to your staff members with a flourish.

Some ideas include
- an all-day retreat
- a guest speaker or mentor
- an intensive educational experience

Or begin as if you are launching a new candidate in a political campaign, and get the word out with the following suggestions:
- Hang signs and posters
- Celebrate the *idea* of your new approach
- Find slogans and catch-phrases
- Create a buzz

Remember to get "out there" with your intent. You can do this by
- bringing in a "prophet" from outside your organization to lend credibility to the vision
- discover who will be your supporters and who will hold you back (give the former free rein, and offer the latter more education and support)
- communicate the vision in pictures, words, charts, and graphs
- find 10 other ways to communicate the vision

These opening gambits create the sense of urgency, a sense of your vision, and a sense of your guiding coalition. They also generate energy to move you forward.

Key points in this chapter

1. Change occurs in stages
2. An assessment of an organization's readiness for change is crucial
3. Change initiatives require constant and consistent leadership
4. The use of data can help educate your staff on the need for change

Building the management team and developing the leadership process

CHAPTER 4

Building the management team and developing the leadership process

A shared vision is not an idea . . . it is, rather, a force in people's hearts . . . at its simplest level, a shared vision is the answer to the question 'What do we want to create?'
–Peter Senge

Now that your vision is established and you have a sense of both where you are going and how you are going to get there, let's discuss building the management necessary to move the initiative forward. To do so, you must

- assess your current management team
- identify strengths and areas needing strengthening
- determine how to rebuild the team if necessary
- develop your leaders/managers
- use focused retreats
- create motivation to change

Assess your current management team

As mentioned earlier, your management team is a crucial component of your success. Team members will help you engage and motivate your work force, build momentum on their excitement and support, and bring their expertise into play to improve on your model/concept. Without them, you will stall and lose your workforce—even if members of the workforce want to change—because they will not want or be able to move forward if their direct supervisors are not on board.

Midlevel managers and supervisors must wholeheartedly believe in and support cultural change for it to take hold. If they don't, they are likely to mount the first wave of resistance to thwart the project. Such resistance comes from fear of new territory, concern about staff objections, and anxiety regarding the skills necessary for a new direction—all under a cloak of, "I don't have time to do that along with everything else I need to do."

Managers and supervisors frequently complain that they spend too much time working

Chapter 4

with staff instead of doing their work. But they are missing the point—working with staff *is* their work, and the way they work with staff is crucial to the work environment.

For these reasons, before you unveil your vision for the entire organization, it is important to assess the strengths of your managers and supervisors and determine whether they are in the right roles to turn your vision into practice. To do so, you need to spend considerable time with your management team to see whether they are up to the task and can support the vision. Using a change readiness tool, as described in Chapter 3, can help you accomplish this important task.

Use focused retreats

Once you decide to roll out your ideas to managers and staff, think carefully about how to do it. Depending on the size of your initiative, you may want to devote a sizable amount of time to or hold a focused retreat for introducing your ideas.

Changing a hospital culture from one of controlling behavior to one of engaging behavior is certainly significant enough to warrant a half-or full-day focused management retreat. In addition, pulling the management team away from the worksite and devoting four to eight hours to discussing your vision certainly sends the message that this initiative is different than those that have come before. Making the initial presentation in a dedicated and deliberate way can help mitigate the influence of those who disengage by thinking or saying, "Here we go again," or, "Another day, another initiative," or "This, too, shall pass."

By using a focused retreat that is designed exclusively for this initiative, you create opportunities to lay out for your management team all of the reasons you have decided to make the change. By presenting your case in a thorough and methodical way, you create the opportunity to demonstrate why it's necessary to change, what the change is, and how the change will take place. If your management team is enthusiastic, you may also hear new ideas and considerations that could strengthen your reasons and improve your plan.

Another benefit of a focused retreat is that it allows you to assess your management team and determine who supports your vision. There may be very good reasons why one or more of your management team objects to your plan, and it will be important to listen to that feedback and adjust your methods accordingly.

Also remember that your management team is strongly invested in the status quo, which reflects their management talents. Sailing off into new waters may produce anxiety and cause unconscious resistance to your new initiative—they may wonder whether they have what it takes for a successful sail. Be aware of that, and act accordingly.

Once you have reassured your management team that your new vision is not a condemnation of their current work but an opportunity to improve what they are already doing, and you're satisfied you have conveyed that message clearly, then take any continued resistance as a warning that you need to have some one-to-one conversations. These conversations may help you fully understand what the obstacles are for a particular member of your management team. Ensure that these sessions end with agreement on a plan of action that keeps your initiative alive and your vision on track.

Once the managers are educated to the vision and have received assurances that executive leadership is in full support of this initiative, you have the beginning of your new management team. This team's major responsibility is to create the process for instituting change and developing a roadmap for its success. The initial work of the management team is to reflect back to the leadership team the difficulties that the proposed change initiative pose for them as managers and what tools they need to start the process and support the staff they manage.

> ### Sample retreat agenda
>
> A focused retreat is a retreat focused on a single item, like a new vision statement that will shape policy and procedures and the way work or service is conducted. A sample agenda for a focused retreat for a new vision for a business, company, hospital, or hospital department may look like this:
>
> 1. Welcome and introductions (CEO)
> 2. Vision, and why we want to go there (CEO)
> 3. Response/reaction/impressions (management team)
> 4. Retool or full steam ahead (management team)
> 5. How to roll out the new vision to staff (management team)
> 6. Teams/task forces (CEO)
> 7. Next steps and next meeting (CEO)

Create the motivation to change

In the past 20–30 years, most employees in large organizations have seen many change initiatives come and go. Used bookstores have shelves of books going back to the 1960s on organizational change. Few of these initiatives ever took root to effectively create dynamic change. Why? Usually because most of the energy regarding the change process focused on the future—that is, where we want to be rather than where we are and how to get to where we want to be.

Chapter 4

Cultures need a reason to evolve and often those reasons come from some sort of threat. The threat can be legal, economic, moral, or political. It can be driven by advances in technology or it can come from a social or political agenda. History teaches us that threats are good motivators.

Once you have identified a reason to change, that reason becomes your motivator. "If we do not change, our customers will go to the competition, and we will go out of business." Perhaps that reason is the economic threat that becomes your motivator, so you develop your change initiative plans along those lines. Note that altruism (i.e., it's the right thing to do) also can be an agent of change, but it has little strength when the going gets tough.

The reason (motivator) will be challenged by those who resist the change, so your leadership team needs to prepare your management team for that challenge. People generally resist change because they do not understand the reason for it, and they fear that they may not have the skills necessary in the new environment. They often suspect that the "real" reason for change is that management wants to cut back, and that if they endorse this change, they may lose their jobs.

In some cases, that may be true.

If it is, know that honesty is the best policy. That is, if there are jobs eliminated due to your change initiative, then, by all means, talk about it in specifics. If you don't, then everyone will think their job will be sacrificed instead of the few that actually will be affected. Your pocket of resistance will grow much larger than you can manage, and your initiative may stall.

Restraint and seclusion initiative

Have the vision
Let's apply this theory to an initiative to change a patient care culture in order to eliminate the use of restraint and seclusion.

Members of the executive leadership team decide they want to change the work culture to engage patients in treatment and to see the use of coercion—exemplified by the use of restraint and seclusion—as a major barrier to accomplishing this goal. They have developed a vision of their hospital or treatment center being restraint- and seclusion-free in three years. They also know that accreditation bodies like the Joint Commission on Accreditation of Healthcare Organizations (JCAHO) have increased their scrutiny on these interventions and are making it quite burdensome for the organization to continue managing patients in this manner.

To pursue its vision, the leadership team takes the management team on a focused retreat during which they carefully explain their vision and ask for full support from the managers. They ask for help to build a plan that supports the vision of being restraint- and seclusion-free in three years.

Building the management team and developing the leadership process

Leadership listens to the managers react to the vision and hears from them what difficulties may be in store as they develop a plan that supports the direct care staff and the people they serve. The leadership assesses which managers are in support of the vision, which ones are not, and which need more individual coaching to get on board.

Develop motivators

The managers work with leadership to identify two significant reasons for the initiative, which become motivators for the process:

1. An economic/regulatory motivator. For example, the JCAHO has increased regulations and called for more oversight (which increases costs).

2. A moral motivator. There is a growing awareness of problems with using restraint and seclusion, including patient deaths and serious injuries to staff and patients involved in the process.

Provide data

The managers point out to the leadership team that they could expect serious resistance in the work force regarding any initiative to reduce restraint and seclusion from multiple groups that will feel more at risk in the workplace. Nurses will feel deprived of a safety intervention, and the physician staff will feel out of control (and will want to support nurses). Administrators will shrink from the controversy, and some patients will complain that hospitals or programs that forgo coercive treatment are caving in to bad behavior.

It is the leadership team's responsibility to supply the management team with the tools necessary to meet this resistance and to help mitigate it with training, data, and support.

For example, training should focus on new ways to work with patients and, perhaps, on environmental changes that aid engagement (more on that later). Present the data that show most injuries to patients and staff occur when staff use physical force on patients. The amount of solid data is beginning to be enough to show that by decreasing the use of restraint and seclusion, violent behavior on hospital wards decreases.

Unlearn old behaviors

Once you manage these initial obstacles, the harder work begins. Hospital staff are taught how to physically manage patients, and patients learn to expect it. Both groups know their roles and expectations. But the implication that "I can control you by force if I decide to do so" is coercive.

By taking away this behavior, staff have to unlearn what has been a constant and always available tool for them, and unlearning a behavior is both difficult and scary. For example, imagine an artist who masters the use of oil paints, develops an allergy to oil-based paint, and is told to switch to watercolor—which she has never used (or liked or respected). She knows how to use oil paints, she knows how to mix them, she knows their texture, and she knows how they sit on canvas. The artist is accomplished and confident with oil painting; she feels safe with oil paint. But now those paints are gone, replaced with new, foreign, thin, and watery colors. She doesn't like them or understand them and feels totally incompetent using them. Before long, she is looking for ways to return to oil paints ("it's only an allergy") and begins denouncing watercolors as "not real art." In the process, she forgets that she is first an artist who chose to use oil paints after discovering her calling.

Support: The learning of a new behavior

Like the artist, management and leadership have to remind staff that they are caregivers first, and now is the time to stop practicing an older model and learn a new one. The time between stopping restraint and seclusion and developing alternatives is a very difficult period, and you must recognize and balance the anxiety of the motivator and the anxiety of the person learning a new behavior. It is during this period staff may feel abandoned and put at risk by leadership. It is when you may hear, "We cannot cave in to the patient's bad behavior," and "You are risking all of the other patients." But you can make the learning less stressful by frequent recognition of new skill acquisition and by rewarding its progress openly. If, however, you don't support the learning and only turn up the heat on the motivator, you begin to grow fearful and dissatisfied staff who struggle, fail, and leave.

How do you support them?

- Recruit them to the vision, provide them with training (and more training), and build learning environments so they do not feel alone.

- Have your team managers and direct care staff work together in the learning environment so that learning becomes a group effort and not a sole endeavor.

- Make sure that all learning tools are shared equally and that the message of the teaching is constant and consistent.

- Provide coaches to all staff who need to learn new techniques, and role-play situations that call for new solutions.

- Build reward programs that frequently reward staff for the progress they make.

- Build staff rewards so that all staff feel recognized when progress is attained. Create a communication tool, like a weekly update, that consistently appears and marks the progress toward the vision and that informs the entire organization of the initiative, maps its progress, heralds its success, and recognizes its champions.

Building the management team and developing the leadership process

Building the management team and developing the support systems to ensure success is the job of leadership. By practicing the suggestions provided here, you will have built a foundation that will give you the stability necessary to support your vision.

Key points in this chapter

Summary

1. Assess your management staff's strengths and needs
2. Use focused retreats to provide vision and reasons for change
3. Develop a plan with input from the management team
4. Build in recognition and rewards to continue forward movement

Components of cultural change

CHAPTER 5

Components of cultural change

Before we choose our tools and techniques, we must choose our dreams and values.
—Anonymous

Leveling the hierarchy

In previous chapters, we have discussed developing and promoting a vision to bring about culture change in the work environment. In this chapter, we begin to discuss creating the foundation of a cultural change initiative.

First, we discuss the issues of power and control and how they work to inhibit engagement and how you can modify your environment without sacrificing safety for patients or staff.

Second, we discuss language and its importance in a work culture (or any culture, for that matter).

Third, we explore the topic of attitude and how to adjust yours to complement the healing environment.

Finally, we talk about changing expectations and beliefs, the beginnings of a "learning community," and how to create new assumptions that influence improved outcomes.

Power and control

Healthcare, especially in hospitals, is rife with examples of power and control inequities. A patient enters a hospital, gives up his clothing, gives decision-making over to his doctor, is at the mercy of nursing staff, lives by the schedule of the organization, eats when food is delivered, gives blood on demand, is wheeled into the operating room at a preset time, and receives medication at someone else's behest.

Chapter 5

In locked psychiatry units, because of tradition and because of safety, a patient gives up even more: belts, shoe laces, headphones with cords, and most personal belongings. He may not have access to mail and may have only restricted access to telephones. Psychiatry inpatients have precious little privacy—many rooms have cameras and speakers. In addition, an overwhelming majority of patients admitted to acute psychiatric hospitals are hospitalized involuntarily.

In such environments, overhead public address systems announce activities and issue directives. Medicines may be given against a patient's will. It is possible—often visibly so—that a patient could be locked in a room in segregation from others or strapped to a bed with leather restraints. Nursing staff members congregate behind high counters or Lexan windows, out of reach.

It is hardly a surprise that patients are prepared to fight for what they want or that they remain vigilant and defensive. Perhaps the surprise is that any patients at all are able to engage in therapeutic interactions under these circumstances. Equally surprising is when staff members are able to engage therapeutically under such circumstances.

We can do better

Xavier Amador (2000) suggests that our mental health system needs to find ways to be partners with those we seek to serve, rather than alienating them, and the first step to such partnership is to level the hierarchical nature of traditional inpatient psychiatry.

Granted, the very nature of a locked unit is one of power and control, but within its walls we can significantly mitigate patients' need to struggle against power and control issues. For example, obvious displays of power, such as the following, do more harm than good in achieving partnership with patients:

- Jingling keys worn on staff members' hips

- Removal of patients' clothing in favor of scrubs

- Institutional signs listing rules, regulations, and warnings

- Interacting with patients only over the protective height of a nurse station counter or through a small speaking hole cut into Plexiglas

- Setting up situations in which patients have to ask for everything they need

Such displays put patients on notice that they are not in control, that they are not competent adults, and that no one expects them to do well. Moreover, these messages reinforce the idea of staff as the decision-makers and the power brokers—and they are often a patient's only avenue to family and the outside world.

Walk in the patient's shoes

Imagine yourself locked away on a psychiatric floor of a large county hospital against your will and feeling powerless about your circumstances. What are the chances that you would comply with the decisions made about you and that you would agree to the facilities' treatment plan?

All healthcare settings have safety as their first concern. As in any setting, we must abide by rules that maintain safety. But as you walk through your facility watching and listening with the eyes and ears of a patient, you may discover examples of power and control. You must identify and eliminate the sources of these spurious shows of power and disrespect to establish the first essential steps in an environment of collaboration.

Language and vocabulary

Culture both reflects and drives values and ideas. Language and vocabulary communicate them. Thus, words we choose to describe our work and the people we serve reveal our biases and perspectives.

Here is a typical chart note in any psychiatric hospital in the United States:

A 45-year-old, white, single, chronically schizophrenic male patient is admitted because of noncompliance with medication and failure in his group home. He was demanding and verbally aggressive with his case manager. He refuses blood drawn in the emergency department (ED) and becomes combative with staff, requiring four-point restraint. He has chronic auditory hallucinations and delusions even at baseline, and he has alienated all of his treatment providers.

What does this chart note say about hope, blame, and expectations? How is this man's illness understood? What is our explanation of his current situation?

Watch what happens to this note when we change keywords and include the patient's perspective:

Mr. Smith is a 45-year-old man who has been off psychiatric medications for two weeks. His mental health support staff member has been unable to ascertain what prompted the discontinuation but reports that Mr. Smith has struggled significantly with side effects of many psychotropic medications, including a 25 lb. weight gain over the past two months. Mr. Smith had hoped to move to independent living until about two weeks ago, when his financial situation changed and he once again was directed to ask his family for support. He expressed reluctance to do so, and alternatives have not yet been explored. He was taken, against his will, to the ED, where attempts were made to force him to give blood, which he is fearful of doing. The mental health agency has not yet discovered an effective way to mitigate Mr. Smith's symptoms of auditory hallucinations or delusions without serious side effects.

Chapter 5

Choose your words
We encourage you to explore your use of these words and terms:
- Behavioral plan
- Privileges
- Levels
- Case management
- Compliance
- Denies/refuses
- Chronically mentally ill
- Time-out

Invite a patient to review his or her medical record with you, or pair up staff members to read a chart together and find language that works well and isn't blaming or judgmental. Also, review your policies and procedures. Does the language in them reflect respect for patients, customer-service concerns for guests, and the value of partnership? Identify the coercive elements and change the wording. How do the policies read now?

Listen to how staff use language
Finally, listen to your staff. How do they speak to each other about their work and those they serve? How do they speak with patients? What is the tone that is used? What are the words that are chosen? If you were a patient/guest, would you find the discussion about you to be respectful and the conversation *with* you to be engaging?

A nurse recently told a story of her hospital's private vocabulary: "When we called someone 'borderline,' it meant we had to spend more than two minutes to meet their needs. We used the term 'schizophrenic' as code for 'won't get better.' "

Twenty years ago, Don Rickels made a career on television and in popular culture with humor that openly degraded women and people who were Polish, Irish, black, or Jewish on every family variety show on prime time. Today, you would not hear anything like that on network television—the culture has progressed. Likewise, we firmly believe that we are in the middle of a healthcare culture that is progressing, and we need to progress with it by reassessing our beliefs and changing our language.

Once your staff members become aware of the power of their words, change will be dramatic. Labels and phrases that were once part of everyday life have become so politically incorrect today that they won't be heard again. And when they are inadvertently uttered, their sound is so jarring as to make you uncomfortable. New vocabulary that sets a tone of respect, dignity, and hope will help your employees become the healers they wish to be.

Attitude adjustment: Serving our guests

Common sense and common experience suggest that when people are treated well, they are better able to tolerate stress and discomfort. Healthcare has lagged behind business in its understanding of the power and importance of customer service.

In psychiatry, and particularly in the Engagement Model, creating an atmosphere that sets people at ease in the context of severe psychiatric symptoms is critical early on. Hospitals need to be more cognizant of the mental state of the incoming patient and understand that no matter how overworked staff may feel, the patient is not thinking of the staff's workload, does not feel that his or her admission is in any way an inconvenience to the hospital, and should never be made to feel that way.

Admissions
Keep in mind that most people arrive at psychiatry inpatient units in considerable discomfort from their own symptoms and having made the difficult decision (or experiencing the consequences of others' decision) to come to the hospital, having experienced perhaps violent police interaction, and often having waited for long and uncomfortable periods of time in an ED. Staff's initial greeting in the form of sincere efforts to provide relief from those past hours can be a crucial turning point in an otherwise bad experience—or it can be a continuation of helplessness, fear, and uncertainty.

Busy, acute, short-stay psychiatry inpatient units often approach new admissions with irritability at worst, hurried efficiency at best. The patient's experience, however, is profoundly altered when they (and family, when possible) are greeted warmly and met with a genuine happiness that the person-has arrived. Have the sole goal of welcoming a newcomer to the environment and a mission to set the person at ease. The components of such a greeting are familiar: standing, smiling, walking toward, touching a shoulder, expression of concern, and offering hospitality. This works in any healthcare setting.

When offered amenities such as food, a beverage, or a warm blanket before admission papers, civil rights notices, medicines, and the demand to strip off clothing, people are much more inclined to engage in the bureaucracy of the hospital and treatment recommendations when the time comes.

Access to what they need
As mentioned earlier, traditional psychiatry inpatient units are structured so that people must ask for most everything—access to a phone or computer, their belongings, food, toiletries, videotapes, personal stereos, etc. Once the environment is changed to allow access to as many of these things as is safe, power and control struggles are reduced. Staff members can then turn the remainder of requests into opportunities to serve.

Also consider the difference for patients when they are proactively approached by a staff member asking what can be done, rather than having to stand in front of a nursing station counter, being ignored and being told they have to wait because of a shift change. Consider the difference in the experience for staff members when there is an attitude of "I'm going to make your day today." Consider the change in relationship when staff members consider patients as guests they are eager to serve rather than as problems they must confront.

This simple but fundamental shift in perspective is a major factor in moving from a culture of paternalism and control to one of service and healing.

Changing expectations and beliefs

People who have worked in the mental health field often fear mentally ill patients, particularly on traditional, locked inpatient units. All employees practice regular exercises in controlling patients' behavior and in deescalation, take-downs, and, of course, restraint and seclusion. Such exercises naturally lead to the expectation of and readiness for people who are dangerous, uncontrolled, and uncooperative—and people often live up to the expectations that others have of them.

Meet me with force and I of course tense up and become defensive.

Meet me with a cup of coffee and a warm blanket and I become more relaxed and receptive.

Meet me immediately upon arrival with a clipboard and 60 minutes of personal questions and I become wary and guarded.

Meet me with an invitation to take a shower or have a bite to eat and I am more likely to answer your questions with clarity and thoughtfulness.

Expectations in the physical environment

Expectations are reflected in the physical environment and in the interactional styles used by staff and others. Many cues are given regarding expectations: Is the physical plant clean and neat? Then newcomers keep it so. Are there bars on the windows? Then newcomers know that attempts to break windows are expected. Is there a fish tank or plants? Are there pictures on the wall? Then newcomers know that aesthetics are important here and react accordingly. Is my first impression a dingy room with a bad odor, broken furniture, and graffiti on the walls? Then I will make my own assumptions (and set my own expectations) of where I am and of the people who inhabit the space.

Expectations in staff behavior

Staff members, too, respond to expectations. When a new patient is anticipated for admission and the situation has been advertised as highly volatile, scary, and associated with a history of requiring restraint, then staff arm themselves accordingly: with adrenalin flowing, a game plan devised to take control, needles ready, a show of force at the door, leather restraints, and take-control attitudes. Nearly any patient (or staff member) will react to meet the clear expectation that one has to fight hard in this dangerous place.

Likewise, when staff members operate with the sincere expectation of tranquility, safety, nonviolence, and respectfulness, patients respond accordingly. Even people with psychosis, substance intoxication, and dementia pick up on nonverbal expectations and cues. During development of the Engagement Model, we were continuously impressed with the effectiveness of culture in eliciting safe, nonviolent, and cooperative responses from all people, no matter the diagnosis, personality structure, history, or symptoms.

When staff members approach the news of a new admission with excitement and eagerness to serve and anticipate it as an opportunity to carry out their mission, the entire tone of the unit changes.

'Learning communities,' rituals, and traditions

Changes in attitude, expectations, and assumptions take perseverance. Many of healthcare workers' behaviors and styles are practically unconscious, so doing old jobs in new ways can be challenging. Another essential component of the new culture, then, is the easy and ubiquitous feedback both among staff members and between staff members and patients that tells them how they are doing.

In addition, modeling new behaviors for each other is a rapid way for the behaviors to take hold and grow. Checking each other's assumptions and expectations builds continuous improvement opportunities. Developing an atmosphere where overt comments on each other's performance are welcome and desired leads to the ability to hold onto gains and mitigate slipping back into previous behaviors.

Scripting learning interactions may help early in the development of learning communities (Senge, 1999). One common technique is to set up admission interviews by assigning one staff member to facilitate the conversation and another to observe with the intent of giving feedback later. The feedback sessions may be structured using specific checklists. For example, what language did the staff member use that was particularly welcoming? Did the staff member remember to offer amenities? Was there any pejorative language used in charting?

Obtaining patient input into the feedback is especially educational. How did the *patient* experience the interaction? When staff members become eager for others' feedback regarding their customer service acumen, new social norms evolve, and cultural change is in progress.

Chapter 5

Celebrations of success and strengths are other key elements in the creation of a community that can honestly assess itself, find faults, and make improvements. Recognition and appreciation of employees' efforts and achievements are prerequisites to staff members' recognition of patients' strengths. In building a learning community, including ritual acknowledgment and celebration helps to shift an organization from reactive to proactive.

Creating new assumptions: Hope and recovery

The Recovery Model has received attention and support over the past decade as consumers and advocates have demanded the right to hope and espoused the importance of autonomy (Munetz and Frese). Traditional inpatient units struggle with the Recovery Model's fundamental notion that responsibility for and control of treatment and wellness lie with the person affected by the illness. Munetz and Frese point out that traditional medical models focus on symptoms, illness, and disability. In the Recovery Model, however, as people become less encumbered by their symptoms, whatever healthcare setting they are in should become less paternalistic and more person-centered.

Patients and staff respond to an environment that assumes that people recover from whatever brought them into the hospital, that mental illness symptoms are relatively minor parts of a person's life (and even less a part of their identity), and that people have many roles outside of their "patientness." Moving from an illness model to an injury model (Bloom, 1997) in this way changes the essential question from "What is wrong with you?" to "What happened to you?" It carries the implicit assumption that whatever happened can be fixed and that a return to regular functioning is not far away. Patients are not blamed or judged regarding who they are but instead are partners with the healthcare staff in figuring out how to recover.

The healthcare setting is, after all, a tool for patients to use in assisting their recovery. It is the role of staff members to ensure that the tool is user-friendly and works efficiently. If the tool is not accessible and does not support the goals of the patient, then it is up to staff members to change the situation accordingly.

For example, if a patient is destructive or violent in the healthcare setting, then perhaps the questions ought to be, "How have we failed to create a user-friendly environment for this individual? What needs have we not met? What cues have we given that are frightening or disrespectful?" When patients who have historically done poorly in hospitals do particularly well in yours, your questions ought to be, "What did we do well that set this person at ease? What is at work in our environment that allowed this person to engage with us so well?"

Key points in this chapter

1. Be aware of elements of power and control and how they affect interactions
2. Review language and how it may be more respectful and representative of your vision
3. Explore how individual and organizational attitudes set tones for recovery
4. Examine how to change expectations toward engagement and recovery

Implementation

CHAPTER 6

Implementation

If we do what we've always done, we will get what we've always got.
—Alan Urbanski

In this chapter, we discuss the challenges of implementing a change model and give you concrete examples of what worked for us and why. We review the physical environment in which you deliver care and the social environment in which your patients and staff interact. We detail our belief in developing a sense of community and the valuable role of the community meeting.

In addition, there are sections on staff-to-staff interactions and staff-to-patient interactions. We ask you to review your admission process and look for ways to improve it to foster increased collaboration and reduced conflict with the people you are trying to serve. Finally, we introduce the concept of a trauma risk assessment and how to use this assessment to improve safety for all members of your community.

Implementing a patient care model similar to the Engagement Model is not as difficult as it may sound. There are few budget implications, and it is hard to object to the core principle of involving patients as partners in planning their care. Embarking on changing a work culture seems daunting, but keep in mind the adage that Rome wasn't built in a day. The initial ideas we suggest to you will produce additional changes that push you even farther along in the process of creating a new treatment arena that supports patients and reduces coercion.

Physical environment

Start by looking at your physical space as though for the first time.

First step: Leave your building
We suggest leaving your building or unit and walking around the block to approach your physical space from a different location than normal. Look at your surroundings. What do

Chapter 6

you see? Is the environment welcoming? Do you feel safe as you approach, or threatened? If patients enter through a different door, imagine what it is like for a family member to approach on their first visit. Pay attention to signage and to the ease of entering.

Second step: Look at the landscaping and the patient pathway

Does the building appear institutional? What does the first sign say? If it is a locked unit, how are the family members treated the first time they arrive? Ask the same questions about the patient pathway. Imagine you are being admitted. What do you notice? Once inside the first door, what do you see as you are met by staff? Is the unit colorful? What do you hear? How does it smell?

Third step: Look at the wall space

Is the wall covered in wallpaper or in paint? What do the signs say? People scan all of this as they are admitted in hopes of seeing something that reassures them they will be safe, respected, and well treated. As you do this exercise, think about what you would want to see and what might help to reassure and comfort you as you enter this treatment environment. Anything and everything you can do at the point of entry to help calm down your troubled patients and reassure them that this is a safe place—a place of hope and healing—will go a long way to address their fears and anxiety. It will help them with their admission and first impression.

This exercise is very important for you and your staff to complete—do not overlook it. This first impression has a way of hardwiring responses, so you have an opportunity here: you can increase stress and escalate a patient, or you can recognize the trauma of admission and redesign the environment to acknowledge that stress and address their often unspoken fears and concerns.

Let us give you a personal example. It wasn't until we were giving a tour to a colleague that we paid attention to the very first sign our patients saw. It read, "Officers, Check Your Weapons Here." Imagine that initial message. People here have guns. Guns are dangerous. This is a dangerous place. We replaced the sign with one that reads, "Welcome to Salem Hospital—A Place of Healing." Quite a different message. Quite a different response may be expected.

Fourth step: Read all signage

Move through your unit and read every sign in it. Do you have several "no" signs, or are they positive and hopeful? The physical environment is a major factor in adding or reducing tension in your patient population.

Reevaluate every visual cue, and decide what fits your new vision, what supports your new vision, what should remain, and what needs to change. Look at your nurse's station "mission control." Does it resemble a fortress, or is it an open, welcoming, reassuring service center to all who receive treatment? If you have a multilingual culture, are your signs in native languages? We know that under stress, speakers of multiple languages often lose their acquired language and instead speak in their native, more natural language.

Figure 7.5 — Examples of formal debriefing questions for staff

- When did anyone first think something was going badly?

- What did people do with that recognition? How was communication?

- In retrospect, what would people have wanted to happen at that point?

- Were there any assumptions or expectations about this person that "came true"? Did those contribute somehow?

- When did most people know something was going badly? How was communication?

- What did you think might happen?

- What feelings were people experiencing at that point?

- What was the interaction with the person at that point?

- How did the team choose who would do what?

- When did the escalation get out of hand?

- In retrospect, was there anything that could have occurred differently at that point?

- Had this person's triggers been predicted? How was that communicated to all staff?

- Had this person's choices of coping strategies been identified? How were they communicated to all staff?

- Which triggers contributed to this event?

- Was rule-enforcement or frustration with staff or unit policies an issue? What alternatives did staff have around that? Was there a power struggle?

- Did customer-service issues contribute to the situation?

| Figure 7.5 | **Examples of formal debriefing questions for staff (cont.)** |

- What was going on in the environment when things started going badly?

- Were any of those things pertinent to this event?

- Was there imminent danger to anyone? When?

- What alternatives were considered and communicated? Were any tried? What were the results? What would you try differently?

- What is the person's trauma history? Did that contribute? Was there reenactment occurring? How was communication?

- What is the person's past experience in hospitals? Did that contribute? How was communication about that?

- What is the person's situation with medication? Did it help or hinder?

- Did we follow our own process and policies?

- How are staff members feeling? What support is needed?

- Has a feeling of safety been reestablished among clients?

- Has a feeling of safety been reestablished among staff members?

- What shall we do next? What new things are in the person's treatment plan?

- What new things are required operationally for the unit in order for this not to occur again? Is there any training that would be helpful?

- Does this event share any characteristics with other similar events?

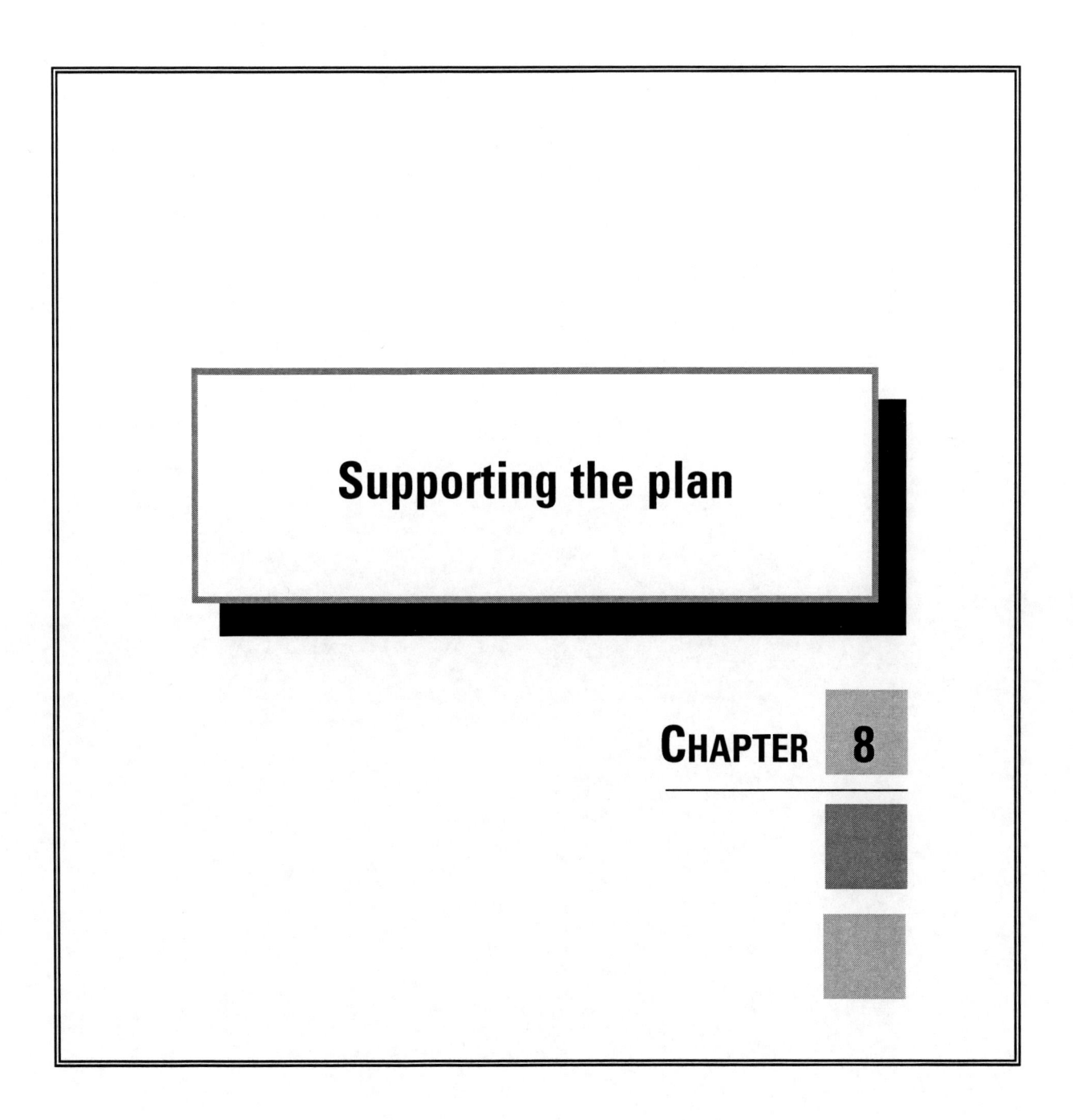

Supporting the plan

CHAPTER 8

Supporting the plan

Culture bearers at all times

After touring the unit where we designed and implemented the Engagement Model and hearing about our success in creating cultural changes, a visiting psychiatrist observed, "This works because you have created a climate of constant change. Your staff isn't intent on a single change; instead, they know that one change leads to another, and somehow you've gotten them into that mode. Don't ever stop changing, because that's when your staff will lose their momentum."

As mental health professionals, we deal in the business of change. After all, change is the goal of therapy, and we know how difficult it is for people to change. When change—or continuous improvement—is built in to our expectations and assumptions, we all get better at it; it becomes a mindset.

Most healthcare organizations find themselves beset with constant change. Leaders must organize these changes into the framework of the vision, clarify the roadmap, and ensure that the changes are understandable and achievable. For instance, when a new regulatory requirement is announced, it is important to translate it into a goal that is consistent with your new culture of noncoercion, patient safety, respect and dignity, and customer service. For example, when the Health Insurance Portability and Accountability Act of 1996 (HIPPA) regulations became law, the scrutiny of patient recordkeeping processes became more intense and overt and were met with skepticism and some disdain by hospital staff. However, by using the language of engagement and customer service discussed earlier, we could reframe these new rules into our model of increased respect and ownership of the treatment by the patient and not the provider.

An e-mail from a hospital in the midst of implementing the model went something like this:

Chapter 8

We admitted a patient three days ago, and he's just out of control. Staff has decided that the only way to manage the situation is to seclude him. We'd been doing really well until now. What shall we do?

The answer to such a question is always to do what you need to do to keep everyone safe. That said, however, there are many opportunities to make progress in the model.

A seclusion following the implementation of the model is an excellent opportunity to learn where and how to focus your improvement process. Ask the following questions:

- How did the admission process go?
- What were the expectations the patient may have had before arriving on the unit?
- What cues did the patient receive about how he'd be treated?
- Were there numerous examples of reassurance and safety?
- Were there environmental and social cues that nonviolence and cooperation are the norms here?
- What are staff members thinking about this person?
- What were the expectations of staff prior to the patients' arrival?
- Has he always needed seclusion?

What have the discussions in community meeting been about? Is there a feeling of nonsafety generally on the unit? What are all the factors contributing to it?

It is essential to take this open, curious approach to every dilemma.

Similarly, how staff treat staff, leaders treat staff, physicians treat staff, etc., are all part of the culture as well. When a physician is rude to a nurse, for example, does the community address the issue? If a staff member errs, does the manager treat the situation and person with respect, dignity, and support? The concept of bearing the culture at all times is essential to the ongoing success of the model. The basic tenets and values must be brought to bear on all situations and on all challenges at all times.

Selecting new employees

As you interview and hire new employees, you have an opportunity to preserve and enhance the new model. Once you have your vision established, and once your management team members know where they are going and that they are supported in taking the organization to this new level, then it is important that all employees be given the same and consistent message that you are changing your behavior and developing new skills.

These new expectations can begin to appear in job descriptions and job announcements. For example, if part of the new culture is that you have established a daily community meeting, then attending those meetings becomes an expectation and, as such, belongs in job descriptions. It can be measured, and it allows employees to be accountable. It can also be a measure of a manager's ability to motivate positive change among his or her staff. If leveling the hierarchy among staff means sharing some duties previously assigned to certain job classifications, then this too can be written into job descriptions. Creating ways for patients to give direct feedback on staff's performance that can be retained and brought into performance reviews gives a clear message to staff that patients are "grading" them on their work attitude and professionalism.

Once you have developed a few of these principles for your existing staff, then you can incorporate these new attitudes and expectations into the job interview process. Here you can discuss the vision and the path you have chosen to make your organization less coercive, and, thus, more engaging for the patient. You can state quite clearly that you believe that with your new vision and principles, there will be less conflict between patient and staff and more opportunity for treatment and recovery. This will be an opportunity to ask prospective employees what they think of your model and how it compares to other environments where they may have worked before. You may be met with resistance, acceptance, or most often, curiosity.

Orienting and training new employees

Once you have hired someone new into your organization, where the new vision already has been explained and new work methods have begun, have your truest believers orient him or her and such new employees should be met with your most enthusiastic supporters (they meet the naysayers soon enough) who can reassure them that they have arrived at a safe place to work and that what your organization is trying to do is both exciting and challenging. To let a new employee be trained by a disgruntled staff member who indicates by word or deed that this new initiative is just a passing fancy is both damaging to your initiative and unfair to the new employee, who is looking to learn and fit in.

We all know a story about the long-standing worker who greets new ideas or new staff with the reprise, "I've seen 'em come and I've seen 'em go. Just keep your nose clean, and you'll be all right." Instead, you want the new employee to reflect your hope and excitement and perhaps begin to influence those existing staff who have been reluctant to lean into the new vision.

Once oriented, employees should have ongoing training and frequent reviews to see how they are doing in this new environment. Begin to hardwire your vision and reassure them that you are interested in their learning and in their feedback as they begin to do their work differently than before.

Chapter 8

As new work processes develop that are in line with your vision, include the new employees in these initial trainings with the existing staff so that their playing field becomes level and they are members of the learning community.

Incorporating physicians

What about the doctors? This question invariably arises during any discussion of cultural change. At Salem Hospital, physicians are all employed hospitalist psychiatrists. As such, the team is small, cohesive, and a captive audience. We found it relatively easy to educate the physicians regarding the vision, use their skepticism as fuel to improve our own thinking, and eventually include them as crucially important culture-bearers and leaders. However, whatever model of physician service your organization uses, you must incorporate, educate, and acculturate the physicians who work there in a planned, strategic manner.

Physicians are, by design or default, leaders. Patients anxiously wait for their daily physician visit, even though the visit may only last a short period of time; nurses take orders from physicians; physicians sign the treatment plans. Physicians, in other words, wear all the accouterments of leadership whether they (or you) plan it that way.

Aligning your vision with your physicians' values and rewards is an important area of attention. The physicians we have worked with are a complex group that is one part conservative, one part traditional, one part oppositional, and many parts focused on helping their patients overcome their symptoms. They thrive on information, choice, autonomy, and incentives. They are intent on using their time and talent effectively and efficiently. They want evidence for new approaches, and they want a clear roadmap for change. Once convinced that a new approach may offer better relationships with their patients and better functional and clinical outcomes, physicians can become your biggest champions.

As your vision approaches its final version, present it to the physicians in your hospital. They will shoot holes in it, but listen carefully, because their perspectives are often clues to the strengths and weaknesses of your plan. Get beyond the change-resistant affect and listen to the content—you'll invariably learn something valuable.

Once you have a plan, invite the physicians to meet with the leadership team and
- give them a clear view of the goal and process
- offer the evidence for your plan
- give them data and articles
- include a physician mentor when you use outside consultants
- outline physician roles carefully

- emphasize their influence as de facto leaders for patients and staff members
- invite their problem-solving skills in how they can use that influence productively
- invite them to participate in the community meeting
- find out what you can do to free up time for one or two docs to attend meetings regularly
- help your hospital devise a way to reimburse them for their time spent engaging in community activities
- invite their leadership in developing staff expertise in the milieu

We knew we were making progress when a senior physician on the unit told us that he'd noticed he now walks around the unit without tensing his shoulders or watching vigilantly for danger. "I just walk around normally, relaxed now. It's a friendly-feeling place. I can pay attention to being therapeutic."

All of this said, there are some doctors who abuse their power, are coercive and disrespectful to both patients and staff, and don't engage with cultural improvements. We suggest leaning into the model to address those challenges.

Key points in this chapter

1. Leaders must continue to be the culture bearers of the change initiative
2. Once defined, new culture expectations become part of job descriptions
3. Use the hiring process to educate new employees about your treatment model
4. Build the model's expectations into new employee orientation
5. Physicians have leadership status and need to reflect tenets of the new culture; use them as culture bearers to help 'hardwire' your model

Accreditation

CHAPTER 9

Accreditation

In this chapter, we look at the various accrediting bodies and how you can develop a culture of continuous improvement that meets the standards of these organizations and keeps your program prepared for any type of review.

Here we introduce our concept of JCAHO Everyday, which we developed in preparation for the Joint Commission on Accreditation of Healthcare Organization's (JCAHO) rollout of it's new tracer methodology and the unannounced survey process.

More than 15,000 healthcare organizations in the United States seek to achieve and maintain accreditation from JCAHO. This accreditation is not required to provide health services, but in order to remain eligible for Medicaid and Medicare funding, organizations and facilities must either be JCAHO-accredited or must pass a survey to meet the Centers for Medicare & Medicaid Services (CMS) Conditions of Participation.

JCAHO standards

In addition to their financial benefits, JCAHO and CMS standards seek to help hospitals improve quality and safety for the people they serve. The JCAHO publishes its standards, which are similar across all settings, in a separate publication for each setting. The publication containing standards for behavioral healthcare, entitled the *Comprehensive Accreditation Manual for Behavioral Health Care*, is more than 400 pages long, so we don't attempt to repeat or address all the standards here. Note, however, that oversight organizations mean well but that they can cripple organizations that get caught up in the rules of compliance rather than understanding the intent of the standard or measure.

Many suggestions in this book enhance hospitals' quality and safety in a manner consistent with JCAHO and CMS standards. In the area of restraint and seclusion, for example, JCAHO standards state the following:

Chapter 9

PC.12.10
"Leaders establish and communicate the organization's philosophy on restraint and seclusion" to all staff with direct care responsibility. This is consistent with creating and communicating a vision regarding elimination of seclusion and restraint and with the value of leadership in such an initiative.

PC.12.30
"Staff is trained and competent to minimize the use of restraint and seclusion and when use is indicated, to use restraint or seclusion safely." The messages from JCAHO clearly indicate that seclusion and restraint must be minimized, and that the organizations must move toward elimination of them in all they say and do.

PC.12.40
"The initial assessment of each client at the time of admission or intake assists in obtaining information about the client that could help minimize the use of restraint or seclusion." The preadmission and admission processes described in this book, along with ever-increasing awareness that a history of trauma or of seclusion and restraint increase the likelihood of seclusion and restraint, are consistent with this standard.

PC.12.120
"Clinical leaders are told of instances in which clients served experience extended or multiple episodes of restraint or seclusion."

PC.12.160
"The client and staff participate in a debriefing about the restraint or seclusion episode." Chapter 7's debriefing description of analysis of restraint and restraint events as well as the immediate inclusion of leadership in the debriefing are consistent with these standards.

PC.12.180
"The organization collects data on the use of restraint and seclusion that are consistent with the importance of an organization becoming data-driven, analyzing in aggregate the factors that lead to restraint and seclusion, and developing action plans that address them."

JCAHO furthermore describes its dimensions of performance, which are characteristics of what is done and how well it is done by the organization. The dimensions will be familiar to you by now:

- Doing the right thing
  - Efficacy
  - Appropriateness
- Doing the right thing well
  - Availability

- Timeliness
- Effectiveness
- Continuity
- Safety
- Efficiency
- Respect and caring

The JCAHO goes on to describe leadership standards that say leaders "establish a planned, systematic, organizationwide approach to process design and performance measurement, analysis, and improvement" and that "activities are planned in a collaborative and, when applicable, interdisciplinary manner." We have simply added to these standards the importance of including the people we serve in these functions.

The standard chapters for provision of care (PC), leadership (LD), performance improvement (PI), environment of care (EC), and use of data (IM) all reflect the principles and processes described in this book.

JCAHO Everyday

Many healthcare organizations have a culture of business-as-usual until a survey conducted by the JCAHO is predicted, at which point the organization goes into a preparation mode that taxes the facility's staff and other resources. At that time, risk managers work around the clock to update policies, consultants are brought in to perform mock surveys and to find where the organization might do poorly, and managers review standards and how their performance compares.

The best way to ensure JCAHO compliance, however, is to develop policies and procedures that are in the best interests of the people you serve, ensure that your policies and procedures are in sync with the JCAHO standards, and then live by your policies and procedures every day—not because you are expecting a survey, but because you seek to operate in a safe, high-quality manner that serves patients, families, and staff in the best way possible. The JCAHO addresses this concern with its new unannounced survey approach and its tracer methodology process.

To stay continuously prepared for survey, we built a response on our inpatient unit that we called JCAHO Everyday. We believe that the JCAHO standards should be seen as minimum standards and that meeting a standard isn't the goal. Rather, we set up the expectation that we would develop a 24/7 culture that exceeded the JCAHO's expectations by being JCAHO-prepared every hour, every day, 365 days a year. You too can develop similar plans. Remember, the JCAHO wants to see you as you would deliver care on any day of the year. If you can develop a culture and inspire a staff to deliver consistently high-quality care all the time, then you can develop a program like JCAHO Everyday—it is simple to design, has integrity, and is what you should be doing anyway.

Chapter 9

The new tracer methodology process works to your advantage with JCAHO Everyday. To build this kind of culture, start with the standards and crosswalk them with your practices. What we found is that we had dozens of time-consuming and often costly practices that were in place because someone believed that they were required by the JCAHO. When we compared them to the standards, however, the requirements were not there. They had developed over time, gotten rooted in our culture, and taken on a permanent place of their own. Just by beginning again, we were able to discontinue many processes, streamline others, and develop new, simpler ones.

For example, our hospital operated under the belief that the JCAHO required a certain staff-to-patient ratio. It doesn't. It does require that certain disciplines be represented by qualified staff, but it does not tie that requirement to the census. We also operated under the assumption that most patient care accessories had to be locked away. They don't. Yet we were tying up valuable and costly staff time doling out toothpaste and shampoo to somewhat insulted patients—all under the guise of "It's a JCAHO requirement."

We were missing the point of the standards and missing the point of the JCAHO survey process. And we were not alone. Hospitals and care organizations around the country are behaving in just the same manner with just the same processes that do not establish a culture of consistent excellent care but rather try to pass the test. We needed to learn the intent of the standards and build a new set of policies and procedures around those intentions.

Once you learn the intent of the standards, you can develop processes that contribute to your overall culture and set the stage for JCAHO Everyday. Teach your direct care staff the intent of the standards—not how to comply with them—for once the intent is learned, then your staff look for related ways to meet that intent and begin to weave the cultural fabric.

A proven way to begin this process is to read your standards in a staff meeting and to discuss their intent. Come to an agreement and shape your policies and procedures to meet that intent. Then, once staff learn the intention of the standard, you are on your way to developing an environment that incorporates those intentions instead of treating them as rules to follow only during the period of review.

JCAHO Everyday in action

Let's take the leadership standards' meaning mentioned above and apply the JCAHO Everyday principle to it:

Activities are planned in a collaborative and, when applicable, interdisciplinary manner.

This standard intends for you to develop and plan patient activities with input from the many areas of expertise available to you. Understanding this intent can drive interdisciplinary planning on multiple levels throughout the patient care environment, and this type of planning becomes part of the JCAHO Everyday culture.

Now let's look at PC.12.160 mentioned above, whose intent is for patients and staff to participate in a discussion pertaining to significant events during the course of the treatment period. Develop policies and procedures that reflect this intention by including patient and staff discussion about significant events pertaining to the treatment community. Now you have brought this standard into play and coordinated it with the community approach talked about earlier—that is, the treatment community and the community meeting. And rather than trying to apply the specifics of a standard to specific interactions, you have incorporated the spirit of the standard into all that you do. It finally becomes a fundamental part of our day-to-day culture.

Key points in this chapter

1. Understand the intent of the JCAHO standards
2. Creating a culture of continuous compliance means you'll always be prepared for any surveying agency
3. JCAHO everyday fits with the new JCAHO unannounced survey process

Lessons learned

CHAPTER 10

Lessons learned

In this chapter, we examine several of the lessons we learned as we embarked on, and continued with, our cultural change initiative. Here we discuss mistakes we made in hopes that you won't repeat them. Recognize that some of these "mistakes" may need to be repeated in different organizations, but perhaps as they are being made, you can find comfort in the fact you can make them, recover, and continue to move forward.

There are always obstacles in the way of change, and even the most positive of improvement models often face some sort of pushback. Indeed, whenever there is a status quo, there are people who feel supported by and comfortable in that environment and who don't want it to change. Our initiative to decrease conflict and increase engagement was met with enthusiasm from the people we serve, wary support from our larger hospital organization, and marginal support from our direct care staff.

Lesson one: Identify your partners

Some of our obstacles were of our own making. We made errors in the beginning by not realizing who our partners were. For example, we neglected to inform our hospital security staff of our new treatment approach, and we didn't even think of informing our human resources department—two vital areas of support that we simply overlooked. Down the road, these mistakes would slow our progress, alienate valuable allies, and consume many hours of administrative time as we worked to rebuild those relationships.

We strongly recommend that you complete a thorough analysis of who your partners are and when and how to include them in your planning.

Strategies
We advise you to include
- all departments that work with your department in the direct delivery of service
- consumer groups and National Alliance for the Mentally Ill (NAMI) (or other national support organizations) so that they may support you if your approach is met with resistance from professional organizations or union groups

Chapter 10

When we developed our vision and built our plan, we knew it would be difficult and, except for a few of the lessons discussed in this chapter, we did a pretty good job of predicting where our resistance would come from. Our hospital—a comfortable community hospital—would receive change as technology advanced, as regulations required, or on occasion, with the arrival of a new physician. It was not the custom, however, to ask staff to acquire new beliefs, change daily habits, practice in a new way, and take increased personal risks in lieu of using potentially coercive treatment approaches. For that reason, we knew that we would need the partnership and support of the hospital's executive leadership, and we received that in 2001.

Lesson two: Gain leadership buy-in

Managers were our next obstacle. To our surprise, they generated the strongest resistance we had to face.

Managers are the owners of the status quo. You must articulate your vision to them so that they understand both why you want to change and that you have good reasons for that change. Our management team was split, with about half who supported our ideas and half who did not. We replaced three key managers within one year, which proved challenging, time-consuming (remember our admission about not having HR on board), and necessary, because unfortunately, we could not convert these three managers to our vision.

Letting managers go often destabilizes staff and can make them fearful and wary, two things you do not want when you are about to undertake a significant cultural change. Therefore, converting managers and key staff is always preferable. If they don't convert, however, they have to leave—you cannot be successful promoting and developing a cultural change without the full understanding and support of the management team.

Once you are comfortable that your management team is in place and that its members understand the vision and why you want to move the organization toward your goals, then you can begin to build a staff education plan. This plan will ensure that every employee knows what the vision is and why you are going forward.

One of the biggest obstacles is when direct care staff begin to challenge the new model as too permissive. Staff will see new, and most often higher, thresholds or tolerance of aggressive behavior. Previous to the new model, an angry affect or threatening comment may have landed a person in restraints or seclusion. The new model takes a different approach to such behavior. It is important to anticipate this development and work with staff to understand that the Engagement Model sees this behavior as an indication that a person behaving in such a matter has urgent needs, and that they must be addressed. A need may not be met but should be addressed to deescalate a behavior and avoid physical confrontation. Developing these types of interventions to implement the Engagement Model becomes another job for the management team.

Strategies

The managers who know direct care staff may have ideas about how to roll out the vision and are your best source of advice on how it may be received. Listen to them. If you do decide how to roll out the vision without them, then you are making them your spokespeople, and they, no matter how well intended, are perceived by their colleagues as just that—a mouthpiece of the administration. If that happens, you risk losing their power as managers and leaders.

If you listen to the management team and support their rollout ideas, you swell your ranks, and managers become invested. They will begin to bring forth the vision with wider support and stronger momentum. This, too, is an important lesson we learned the hard way. We started by charting the entire course without managers, had them implement our ideas, and lost 12–14 months in the process.

Once you have managers on board, and they have decided on a rollout plan that you can support, let the management team loose and coach them. As they begin to explain to direct care staff the vision and the why, they will elicit staff support for the changes needed or steps of implementation, which increases buy-in and allows for ownership of the new direction.

For example, if a housekeeper notices that most patients request a second pillow after a day or two on the unit when they feel more comfortable asking for things, then perhaps a second pillow could be offered upon admission. This simple step empowers and engages the housekeeper in your new customer service vision, makes a piece of it their own, and is appreciated by the patients you serve. It also addresses a direct care issue that a medical director or administrator would never be aware of. In addition, acknowledgement from management will encourage this housekeeper to continue practicing the vision, and his or her colleagues will follow suit.

Another example: Food is often locked up overnight, and night staff cannot feed a late-night admission. Having food available allows the night staff to be good hosts, decreases the chances of a conflict, and contributes to the vision of your treatment arena as a healing place. We all know that someone admitted in the middle of the night has probably had a difficult couple of hours, if not more, and often has not eaten in a while. It is simply amazing what a pillow and a sandwich can do to make someone feel welcome and safe.

Once you have moved through your management team and direct care staff, return to the consumers of your services. Share the vision that has been built from those early conversations with them and that has grown as it has moved through your management group and your treatment staff. Have the managers coach treatment staff in using the community meeting to talk about the vision of decreasing coercion, and ask them to help you design the perfect unit.

Chapter 10

Lesson three: Involve the payers

At some point, your payers may hear about your new treatment approaches and may have ideas of their own. If you are embracing a coercion-free environment, then the issue of forced medication is bound to come up. HMOs and MHOs have been known to request aggressive use of medicine to achieve symptom relief and shorten hospital lengths of stay—but they don't pay attention to the trauma issues involved when you force people to take medicine against their will. Although forced medication may expedite symptom relief, it is often an area of conflict that decreases the opportunity for engagement and frequently leads to aggression. Therefore, talk with these partners and explain to them that only through engagement can you make the progress necessary for patients to understand their illnesses and to support their treatment program.

We believe that both avoiding the conflict that comes from coercive medicine and concentrating on engagement can help you obtain a treatment agreement, thereby increasing the chance of treatment fidelity and reducing the risk of treatment failure. If your "funders" support you during a trial period, then you should be able to show them positive results in 90–120 days with improved outcome data showing a decrease in recidivism to the inpatient environments.

Lesson four: Predict uncertainty

As various hospitals and organizations have adopted The Engagement Model, each has arrived at situations in the midst of their cultural change when the best course of action is not clear. As mentioned in Chapter 3, there is a Neutral Zone in which the complete cultural change is not yet quite in place yet the old ways are no longer comfortable. This time is particularly vulnerable, both for the change process and for the safety of staff and patients.

An example is a unit that is not yet stabilized as a healing environment when staff are newly trauma-informed and reluctant to use the old mode of immediate hands-on action, no one knows just what to do with an upset patient. Leadership must predict this moment with staff as the change initiative progresses. They must give full support for ultimately keeping the unit and all people on it safe. Staff ought to be educated about such a time, when their old instincts fail them, new options are not yet hard-wired, and there is danger present.

Restraint and seclusion, or whatever means staff members have historically used to attempt to keep people physically safe, cannot be forbidden by leadership, even subliminally, until the new culture is in place and functioning.

Lesson five: Take advantage of collateral benefits

In 2001, we started out with the idea of reducing conflict by reducing the coercive elements present in our inpatient treatment program. Starting with our physical plant, our policies and procedures, and our personal practices, we reviewed all of our interactions.

Because restraint and seclusion were two of the practices most disliked by both patients and staff, we asked the question of both parties: What do you need to improve this interaction? In the beginning, the question alone triggered enough thought for the incidents to drop dramatically. As the numbers continued to fall, we reinforced every attempt to do something engaging other than restraint or seclusion.

As staff became more creative with their engaging techniques (such as eating lunch with patients), we noticed that the number of adverse incident reports began to decrease as well. Patient satisfaction scores increased, as did staff satisfaction scores.

- Because we were arguing less and engaging more, patients responded to treatment in a more positive way.

- As treatment response improved, length of stay decreased, and our monthly financial picture improved dramatically.

- Because patients became more engaged in treatment, the use of medications decreased (not just "anxiety prn" medicines but all medicines) by more than one-third, as prescribed by our inpatient physicians.

- Because restraint and seclusion often requires combat, injuries to both patients and staff decreased from dozens per year to zero.

- Loss of work days due to staff injuries from restraint and seclusion were eliminated.

- With fewer staff out injured and fewer confrontations at work, staff called in sick less often, and overtime costs were reduced by more than 40%.

- We eliminated the use of "agency" nurses or "travelers" to meet our nursing needs, and when we posted an open position, it became immediately filled—an unheard outcome just a few years earlier.

- Recruitment improved as the word spread that our facility didn't use restraint and seclusion.

Chapter 10

Although many of the above benefits are good news for the organization and the people who work at the hospital, the most satisfying results came from the people we serve. Throughout Oregon, when individuals ended up at crisis centers or emergency rooms and needed psychiatric hospitalization, they frequently asked to be sent "to that place that doesn't lock people up in little rooms or tie them to their beds."

Key points in this chapter

1. Identify all your partners as you design a change model
2. Secure full support of your management team
3. Involve managers in designing a rollout plan to staff
4. Inform your financial partners regarding your new approach to treatment in order to gain their support
5. Look for and champion the collateral benefits of your change initiative

Summary

Chapter 11

Summary

The simple beauty of the Engagement Model is that in any system where a person's civil rights are often relinquished and where one can be detained and medicated against one's will, there needs to be an avenue of hope and respect that leads out of that darkness to recovery. In our work to improve the hospital experience of the people we serve, we began in January 2001 to take apart the traditional model of inpatient care and to build a new model that incorporated the groundbreaking work of Sandy Bloom, MD, and Xavier Amador.

These two thinkers provided us with the impetus and the courage to challenge the status quo and to develop a new approach to hospital care with the patient as a full partner in his or her treatment. We named this approach the Engagement Model. Bloom teaches us the importance of safety and sanctuary, and Amador teaches us the importance of humanity. Our goal was to combine these two values in our direct clinical work with those suffering from symptoms of mental illness.

What we have done is craft a model that fits into this continuum of care and leads from safety and engagement to recovery. Illness requires some type of treatment, and for the treatment to be effective, it must be delivered safely, respectfully, and humanely. The Engagement Model describes how this treatment gets both delivered and received. Once the illness is properly understood (i.e., diagnosis and trauma assessed) and the environment of care is determined to be both safe and sane for treater and treated alike (Sanctuary), then the process of engagement begins with the cooperation and collaboration of the person providing treatment and the person receiving treatment. By addressing and limiting the elements of coercion so strongly evident in the mental health system, you begin to move from a hierarchical, threatening model of care to one of cooperation and engagement. By engaging in the agreement and in working together to remove or reduce debilitating symptoms, you have begun to forge an alliance that improves the opportunity to create true recovery.

Chapter 11

In this book, we set out to do two things:

1. To introduce the concept and chart the course to engagement by addressing the most oppressive elements of coercion (i.e., restraint and seclusion). Review your environment for subtle but persistent elements of coercion that populate your language, your policies/procedures, and your personal interactions.

2. To convey our experience of taking a traditional inpatient program where two-thirds of the patients are admitted involuntarily and apply the principals of engagement outlined in the proceeding 10 chapters. Our plan was not only to convince and convert you to this way of thinking but also to give you solid evidence of its effectiveness. In one of our most difficult years, we had more than 365 seclusions, each lasting an average of more than 10 hours per incident. We had more than 100 episodes of leather restraints. As of this writing (May 2005), we have had one incident of seclusion in the past 24 months, which lasted for less than 15 minutes, and no incidents of restraint use during three years.

We are proof positive that the Engagement Model works and that the use of seclusion and restraint can be eliminated and replaced with treatment interventions that engage the patient and contribute to the therapy of recovery.

In the past two years, we have been asked to consult and train mental health workers from Alaska to New Jersey in a variety of settings and found that when the principles that we have outlined are understood and endorsed, you can expect dramatic success. We know this model to be effective, to be efficient, and, most of all, to be hopeful both for the recipients of our care and for those who provide that care.

We wish you the best of luck with the thoughts presented here, and we encourage you to contact us if we can be helpful.

Tim Murphy, MS
tim@evolutionsinhealthcare.com

Maggie Bennington-Davis, MD
Maggie@evolutionsinhealthcare.com

The Engagement Model: A quick reference guide

APPENDIX

The Engagement Model: A quick reference guide

Introduction

Salem Hospital psychiatry inpatient unit changed its environment of care beginning in 2001. As a result, use of locked seclusion and mechanical restraint has been nearly eliminated. Using a defined vision and strategy, the leaders of the unit sought to change a traditional, involuntary, and often coercive inpatient culture to one of nonviolence, collaboration, and partnership. Unanticipated benefits accompanied the dramatic reduction in seclusion and restraint, including increased patient, family, staff, and physician satisfaction; reduction of patient and staff injury; and improved recruitment and retention of staff and physicians. The core of the model is one of therapeutic community, as described by Sandra Bloom, MD. In addition, by focusing on respect and dignity and seeking to satisfy those we serve, the environment became one of participation and healing. Staff time is used more efficiently, and the program has improved financially.

Demographics

Salem Hospital is a nonprofit regional hospital with approximately 280 beds in operation. The psychiatry inpatient unit is housed in a free-standing building three blocks from the main hospital. Inpatient psychiatry is an acute adult and geriatric, locked, secure unit of 24 beds, with an average length of stay of eight days and a census that is nearly always at capacity. One-third of people admitted are experiencing their first psychiatric hospitalization. People are admitted acutely from emergency departments at Salem Hospital and other hospitals from around the state, med-surg floors, jail, therapist and physician offices, crisis centers, and directly from home or the streets. There are no exclusionary admitting criteria except for acute and active severe physical illness or acute intoxication requiring medical intervention. Primary diagnoses are schizophrenia or other psychosis and mood disorders. Of people admitted, 50% have coexisting substance abuse conditions. Payers include Medicaid, Medicare, and private insurance, and some patients have no means of payment.

Cultural change

In early 2001, the medical director and administrative director of the unit created a vision of noncoercive treatment. Using the trauma-informed theory and approach of Sanctuary

The Engagement Model: A quick reference guide

(Sandra Bloom, MD), the early psychosis work of Patrick McGorry, MD, and the patient-centered thinking of Fred Frese, PhD, and Xavier Amador, PhD, a specific approach to the environment of care was designed.

The leaders focused first on the management team, patients, and families who helped to create a strategic plan to move the unit to a new service approach to patient care. This design team brought in mentors and experts to educate staff members. They challenged and modified basic assumptions regarding ability and violence, reviewed and revised language and vocabulary, and revived respectful and dignified behaviors among staff and patients. They assessed and improved the physical environment. They emphasized the absence of violence in behavior, attitude, and language.

Components of change

Physical plant
The basic layout of the inpatient unit was not subject to change, but new wallpaper was installed, comfortable and inviting common-room furniture replaced institutional pieces, and warning or "no" signs were replaced with inspirational posters and pictures. Staff grouped furniture invitingly and conceived a comfort room. They posted the statement of nonviolence in hopeful font throughout the unit.

Staff deployment
Staff members were given incentives to be among patients rather than behind the counters of the nursing station or in offices. As much as possible, all work was done in the common areas of the unit.

The unit paid for meals when staff members chose to eat alongside the patients from the small kitchen that serves the patients. Normalizing conversation during mealtimes was encouraged and adopted.

Leadership and customer service
The leaders adopted a model of interaction among staff to create an atmosphere where all employees and physicians felt safe, involved, creative, and hopeful. They applied the Walt Disney Co. approach to being "on-stage." In it, interactions among staff are as important and orchestrated as interactions between staff and patients.

Language and vocabulary
Staff carefully analyzed language and vocabulary use, both written and verbal. Patients participated in many group exercises that examined written medical reports and found examples of language use in conversation that gave either a hopeful or stigmatizing impression. Less stigmatizing, less judgmental alternatives replaced words and phrases like noncompliance, time-out, training, case management, denies, alleges, claims, and refuses.

Appendix

Rituals and traditions
Setting and meeting goals, arrivals, departures, successes, and failures all became topics of discussion and reasons for celebration or other rituals. The organization became data-driven, financial and performance indicators were distributed to all staff, and the organization developed a shared vision. Staff posted goals regarding reduction of coercion and discussed them with patients and families, as well as progress toward goals.

Community meeting
All staff, physicians, and patients were invited to participate at least twice each day in community meeting, during which the group reviewed the nonviolent goals of the unit, reviewed non-violence definitions and principles, and solicited discussion regarding current feel of the unit. Behavior and interactions of both staff and patients were frankly discussed in terms of contributing to either the good feeling or not-safe feeling of the moment. The group aired or discussed any events of import on the unit or in the news. They brainstormed game plans for improvement of the current community.

Intensive analysis of seclusion and restraint

Every episode of seclusion or restraint was treated as a system's issue. Staff notified the medical director and administrative director in the moment, any time, 24/7. One or the other or both responded in person, immediately gave attention and concern to involved staff members, and always began with an apology: "I'm sorry this happened to you. I know you do your best work given whatever situation we ask you to take on and given whatever tools we've provided for you. When something like this occurs, I know it is because we have not yet figured out all the resources you need in order to prevent this from occurring. Help us figure out how to not allow this to happen again."

Then the director met with the patient in the moment, again apologizing: "I am very sorry this happened to you in my facility. Staff members do the best they can, but they are limited by the training and information I provide to them. This is not their fault—it is my fault. This is a traumatizing event for you, and I am going to do everything I can to mitigate its long-term effects on you. At some point, I will ask for your input on what we could have done differently. Meanwhile, are you comfortable? What can we do to help you feel safe again?" Both staff and patients debriefed the incident after the fact and brainstormed to identify where in the system we failed. No staff person is ever blamed as an individual.

Trauma-sensitivity
The neurobiology of trauma is carefully taught and retaught from the perspective that people coming onto the unit have heightened vigilance, increased adrenaline flowing, fear that interferes with clear cognitive processes and impulse control, and interference with verbal processes. Staff look to

The Engagement Model: A quick reference guide

the environment for reduction of this revved-up autonomic nervous system, including tone of voice of the receiving staff, offers of amenities, and nonverbal signals of either danger or safety.

Admission process
The admission process, down to the script that staff uses, decreases fear and anxiety, offers service rather than making demands, and puts people at ease instead of increasing their need for defense. Nonverbal signals reassure people, families are included whenever possible, and staff recognize when people are not thinking clearly and need more reassurance rather than direction.

Physicians
Physicians are recognized as influential leaders and community members and are incorporated fully into the model. We understand that physicians who are not aligned with the vision may inadvertently (or purposefully) sabotage the entire culture. Good physician–staff behavior and physician involvement in community meeting and meals with patients and noncoercive interactions at all times are the norm.

Replication
The two directors of this program have provided consultation and support to numerous other organizations and hospitals. This model has proven operational and replicable.

Sample nonviolence statement

This hospital is a place to heal. To be a healing place, we all will work to keep this a nonviolent environment. We ask that we all avoid violence in any form. Violence is not an acceptable behavior in this community.

Violence includes: acts of hitting, verbal abuse, bad language, threats of violence, hurting yourself, or making anyone a victim of these behaviors in any way.

With this expectation, then we can all make this place a safe place that has a sense of security and trust.

Appendix

Figure A.1 — **Seclusion events at Salem Hospital, 1995–2000**

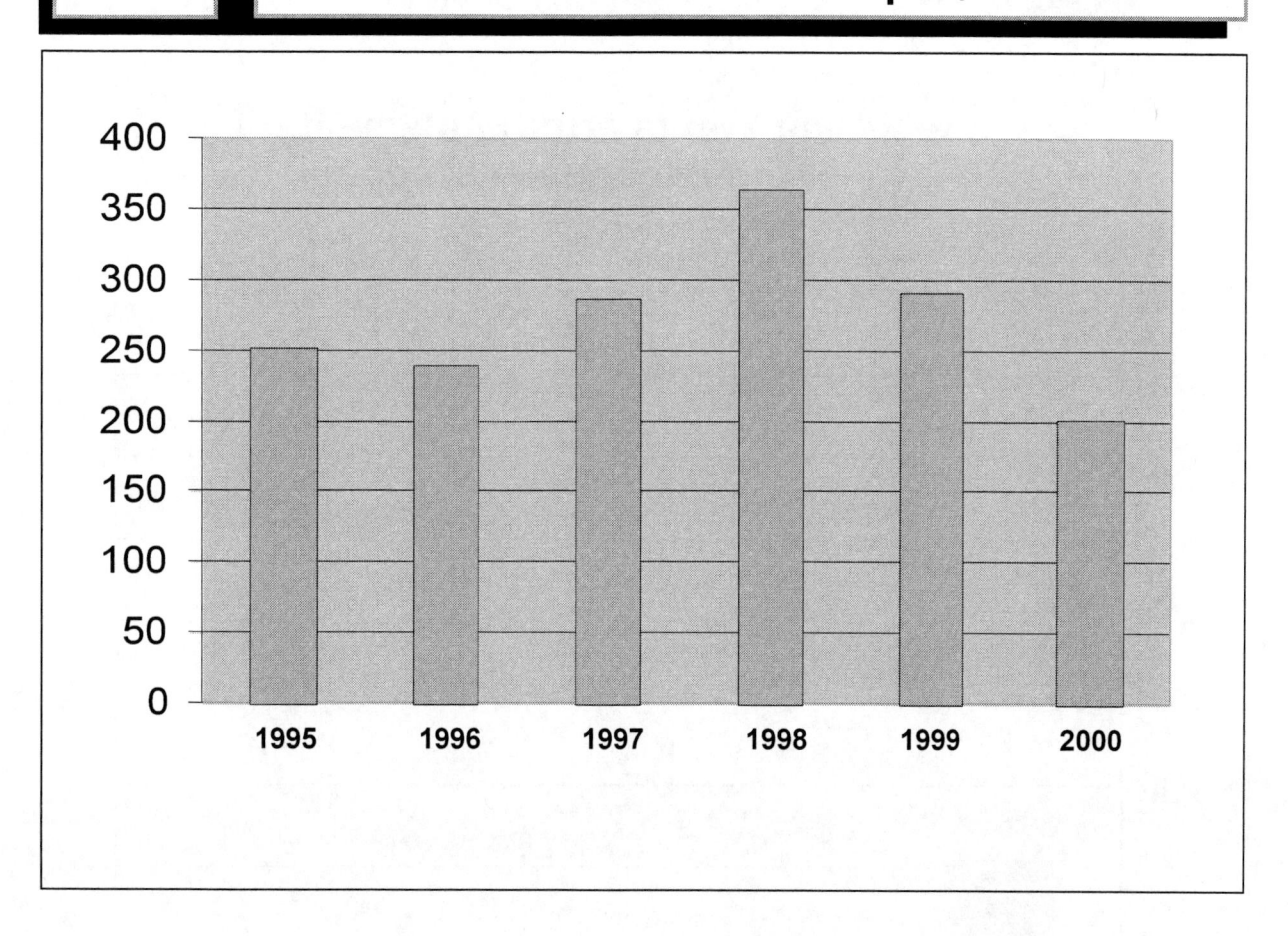

Restraint and Seclusion: The Model for Eliminating Their Use in Healthcare

The Engagement Model: A quick reference guide

Figure A.2 | **Seclusion events at Salem Hospital, 2001–2005**

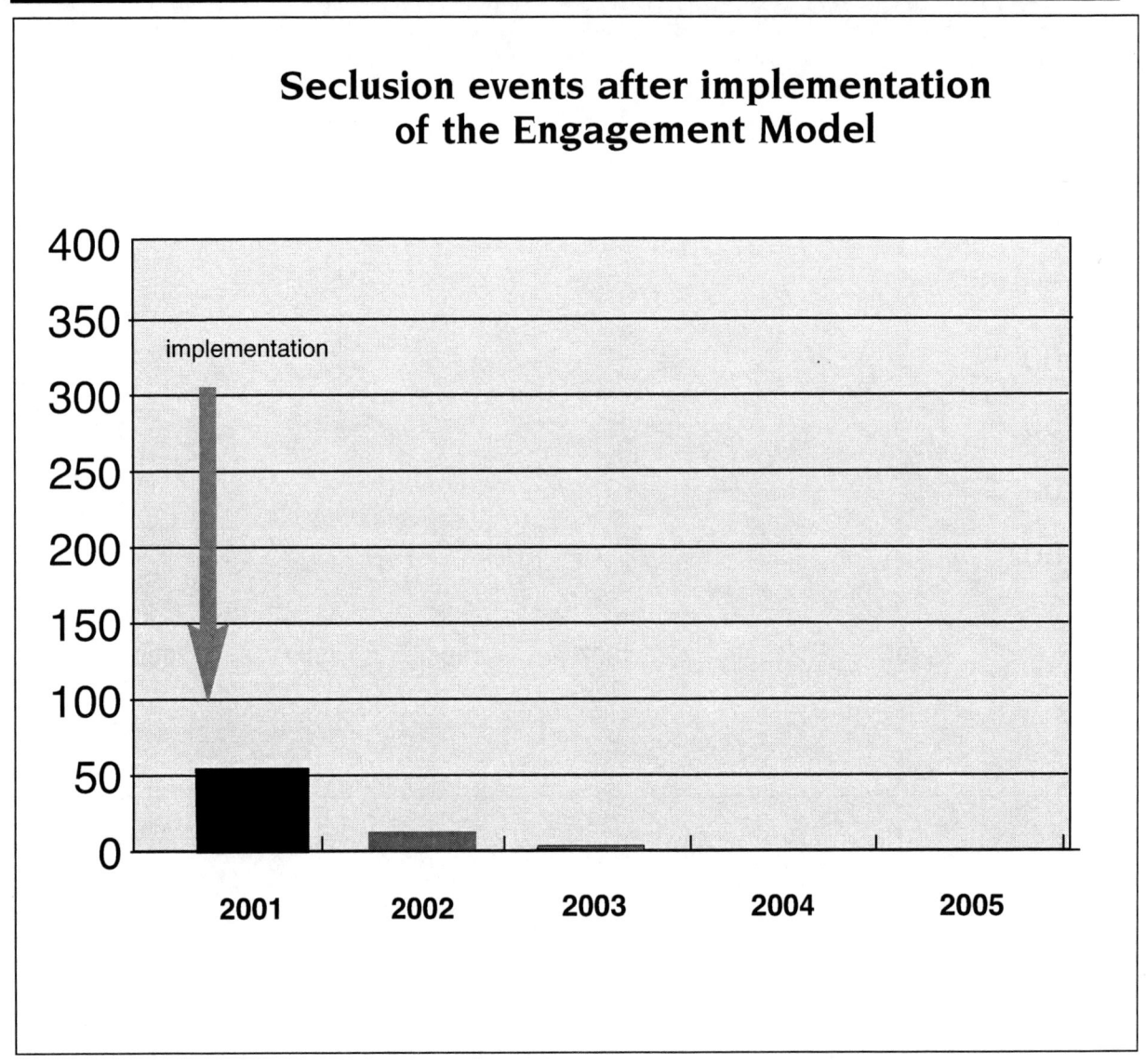

Seclusion events after implementation of the Engagement Model

Year	Events
2001	~55
2002	~12
2003	~3
2004	0
2005	0

implementation (arrow indicating drop from ~300 to ~100)

Appendix

Figure A.3 — **Annual hours of locked seclusion at Salem Hospital**

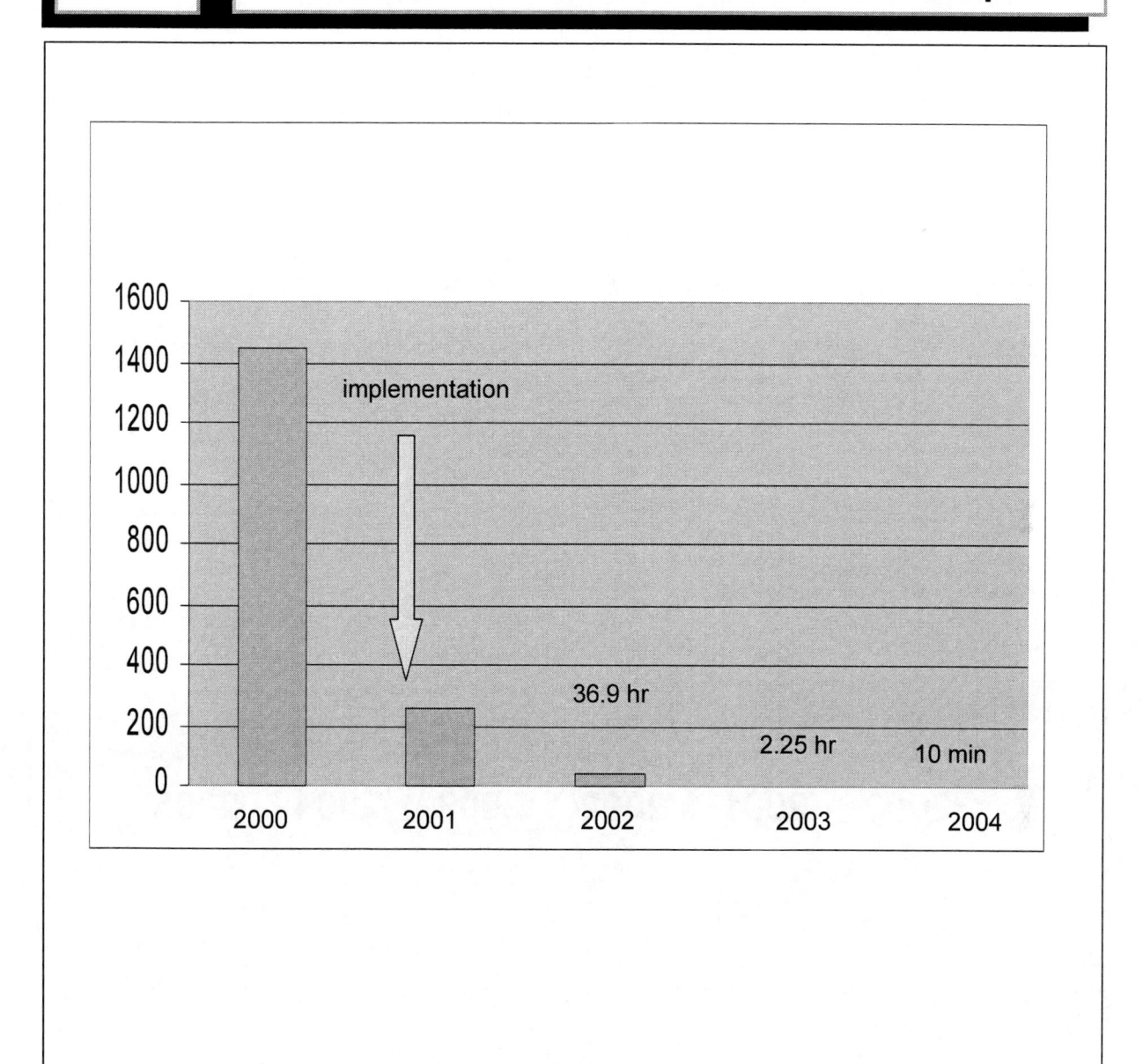

implementation

36.9 hr
2.25 hr
10 min

2000 — 2001 — 2002 — 2003 — 2004

Restraint and Seclusion: The Model for Eliminating Their Use in Healthcare

The Engagement Model: A quick reference guide

Figure A.4 — Employee injuries at Salem Hospital

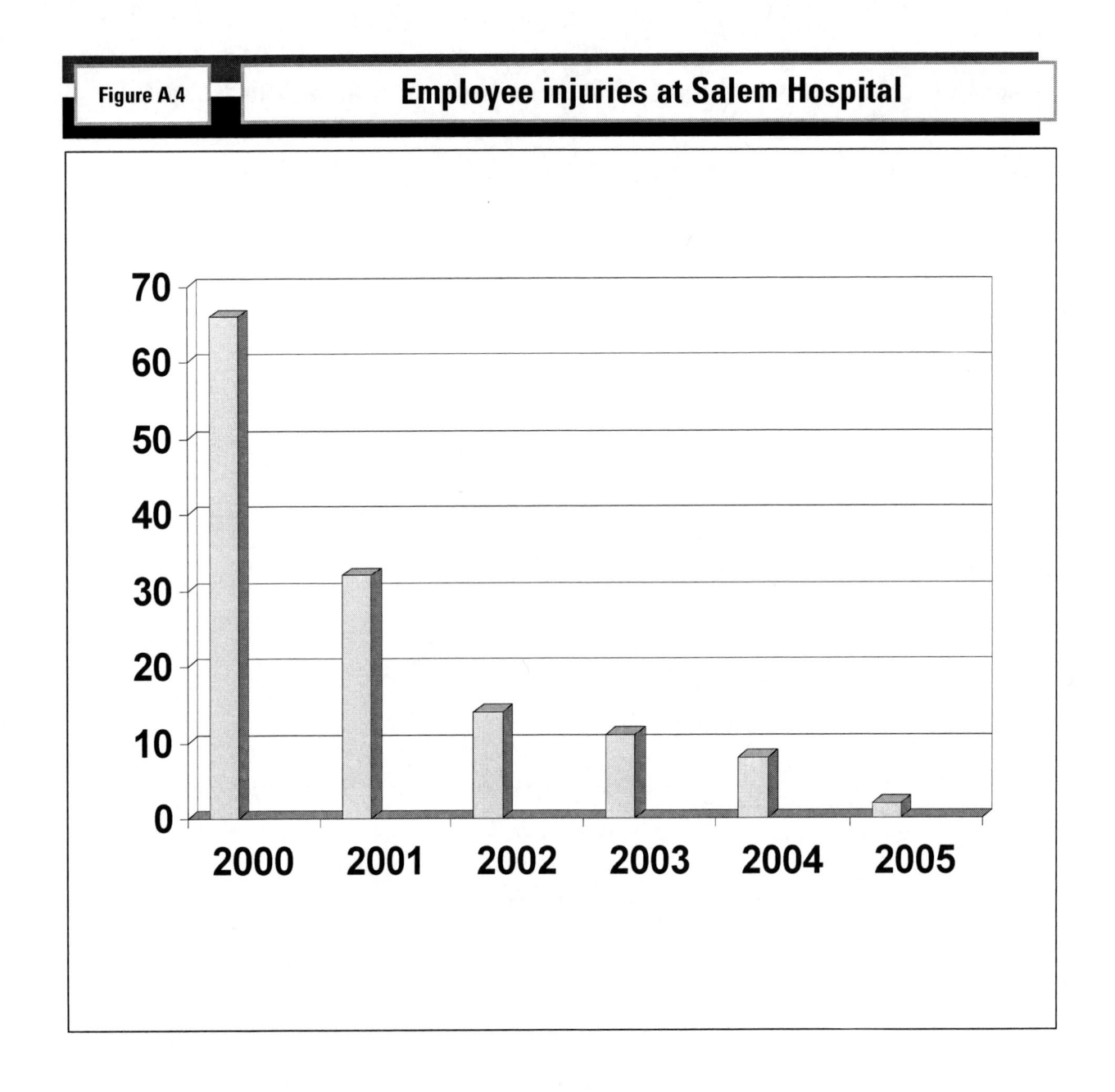

Year	Injuries
2000	65
2001	31
2002	13
2003	10
2004	7
2005	2

Appendix

Figure A.5 — **Cost of workers' compensation claims at Salem Hospital**

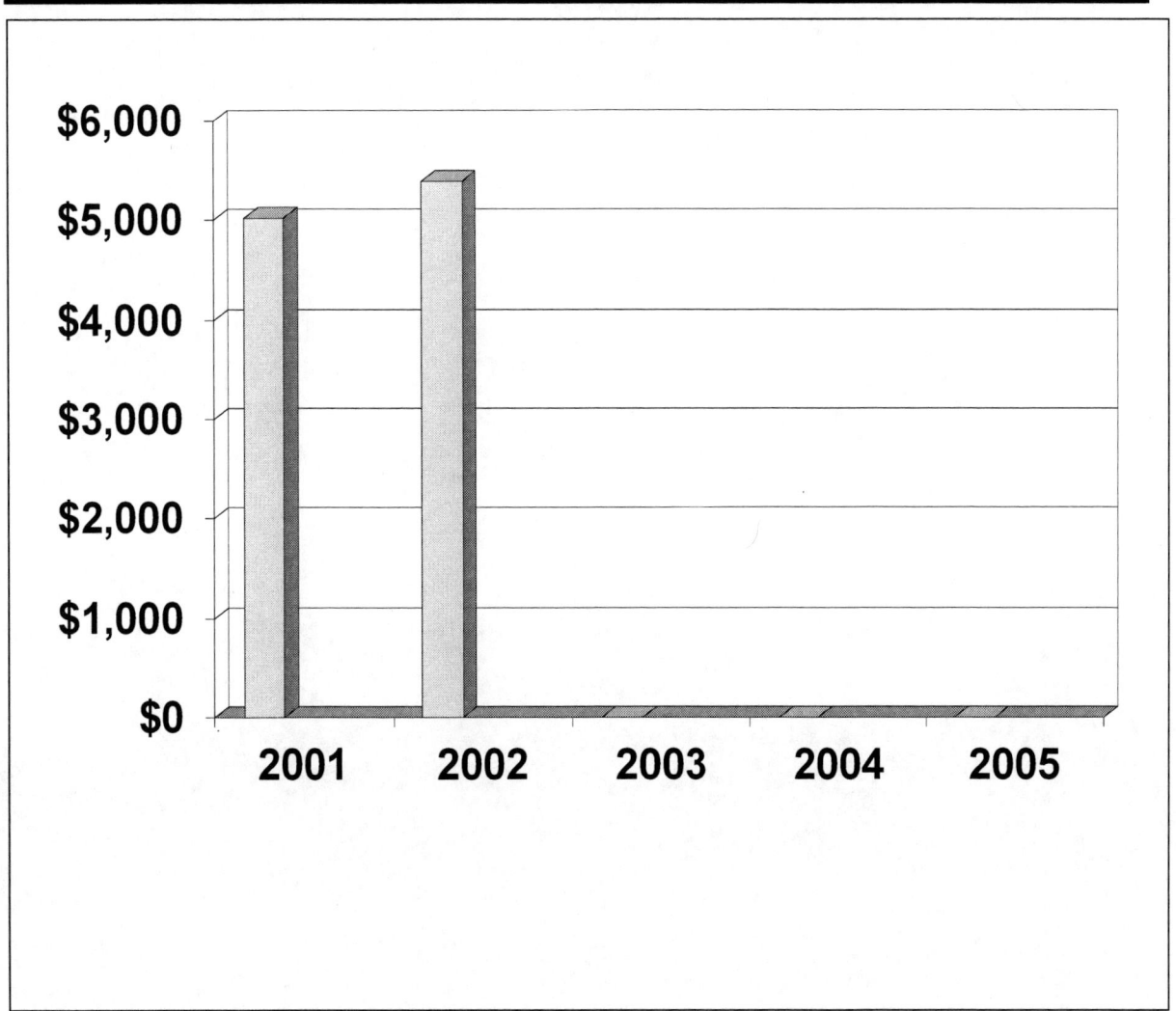

Restraint and Seclusion: The Model for Eliminating Their Use in Healthcare

113

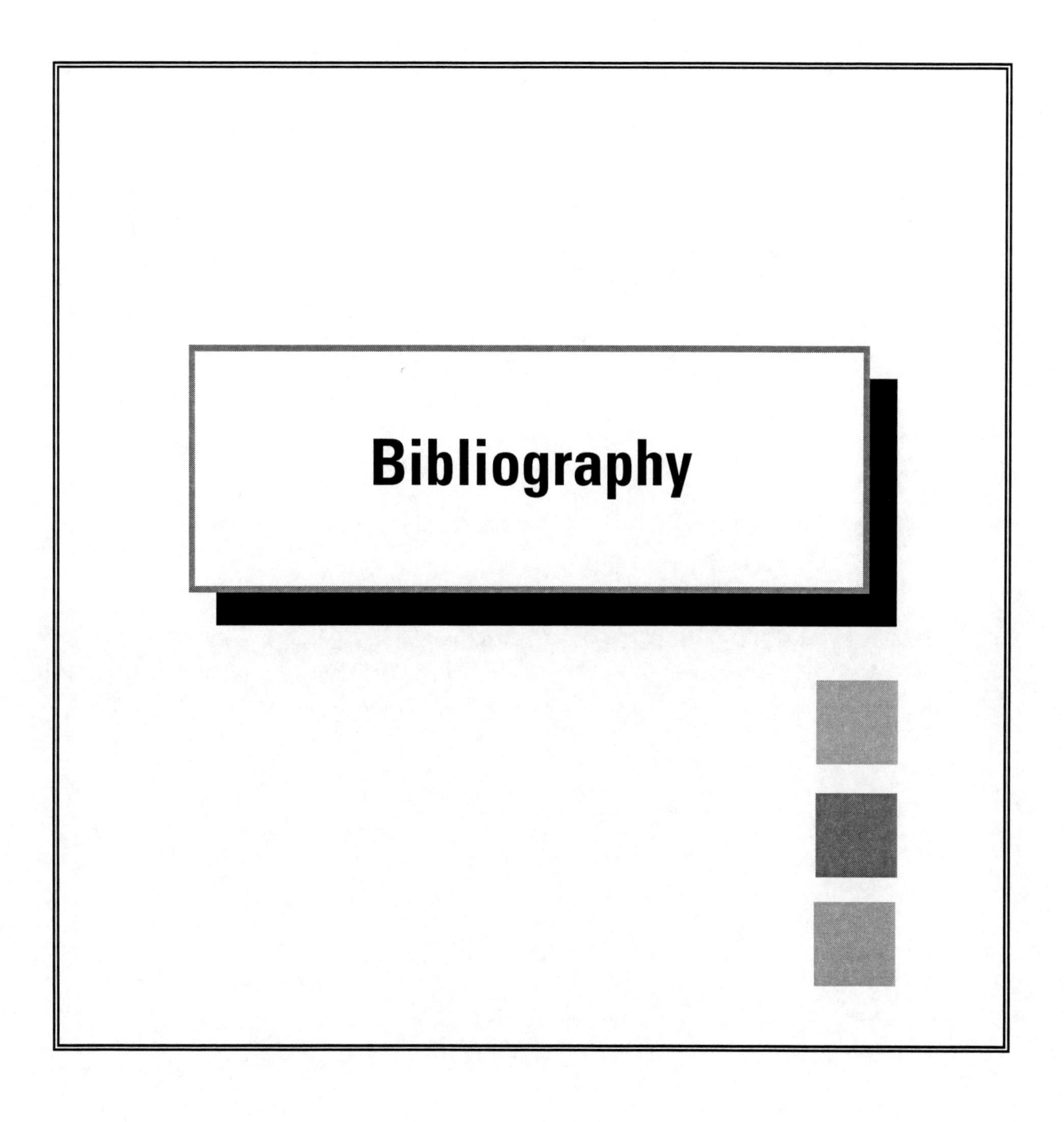

Bibliography

Bibliography

Amador, Xavier. 2000. *I Am Not Sick, I Don't Need Help*. Peonic, NY: Vida Press.

American Psychiatric Association. 1994. *Diagnostic and Statistical Manual of Mental Disorders*. 4th ed. Washington, DC: APA Press. www.psych.com

Bloom, Sandra. 1994. "The Sanctuary Model: Developing Generic Inpatient Programs for the Treatment of Psychological Trauma," in *Handbook of Post-Traumatic Therapy: A Practical Guide to Intervention, Treatment, and Research*. Westport, CT: Greenwood Publishing Group. 474–491.

Bloom, Sandra. 1997. *Creating Sanctuary: Toward the Evolution of Sane Societies*. New York: Routledge.

Bridges, William. 1991 and 2003. *Managing Transitions*. 2nd ed. New York: Da Capo Press.

Collins, Jim. 2001. *Good to Great*. New York: HarperCollins Publishing Inc.

Cook, J.A., J.A. Jonidas, and A. Laris. 2002. *Increasing self-determination: Advance crisis planning with mental health consumer inpatient and other settings*. Chicago: University of Illinois at Chicago Mental Health Services Research Program.

Fallot, R., and M. Harris. 2002. Trauma Informed Services: A self-assessment and planning protocol 1–5. Unpublished papers. Washington, DC: Community Connection.

Felitti, V.J., R.F. Anda, and D. Nordenberg. 1998. "Relationship of Childhood Abuse and Household Dysfunction to Many of the Leading Causes of Death in Adults: The Adverse Childhood Experiences (ACE) study." *American Journal of Prevention Medicine* 14: 245–258.

Hill, R.G. 1838. Total Abolition of Personal Restraint in the Treatment of the Insane. Classics in Psychiatry. Lecture delivered at the Mechanics' Institution in Lincoln, England. Quoted in *Classics in Psychiatry* (Arno Press Inc.,1976).

Bibliography

Hodas, G.R. 2004. Understanding and responding to childhood trauma: Creating trauma-informed care. Pre-press paper. Alexandria, VA: National Technical Assistance Center.

Jennings, A. F. 1998. "Women's mental health services: A public health perspective." In B.L. Levin, A.K. Blanch, and A. Jennings (Eds.). *Being Invisible in the Mental Health System* 15: 326–347.

Kotter, John. 1996. *Leading Change*. Boston: Harvard Business School Press.

Mann, L.S., T.N. Wise, and L. Shay. 1993. "A prospective study of psychiatry patients' attitudes toward the seclusion room experience." *General Hospital Psychiatry* 15: 177–182.

Martinez, R.J., M. Grimm, and M. Adamson. 1999. "From the other side of the door: Patient views of seclusion." *Journal of Psychosocial Nursing* 37 (3): 13–22.

Mohr, W.K., T.A. Petti, and M.D. Mohr. 2003. "Adverse effects associated with physical restraint." *Canadian Journal of psychiatry* 48 (5).

Muesar, K.T., L.B. Goodman, S.L. Trumbetta, S.D. Rosenberg, F.C. Osher, R. Vidaver, P.L. Auciello, and D.W. Foy. 1998. "Trauma and posttraumatic stress disorder in severe mental illness." *Journal of Consulting and Clinical Psychology* 66: 493–499.

Munetz, Mark R. and F. J. Frese III 2001. Getting Ready for Recovery: reconciling mandatory treatment with the recovery vision. *Psychiatric Rehabilitation Journal* 25: 35-42.

Najavits, L. Seeking safety. *www.seekingsafety.org/3-02%20arts/training%20in%20SS-s.pdf* (accessed January 17, 2003).

National Executive Training Institute 2002-05. Creating violence free and coercion free treatment environments: reducing the use of Seclusion and Restraint. A NASMHPD Training Curriculum, Alexandria, VA: National Technical Assistance Center.

NASMPHD (National Association of State Mental Health Progress Directors) *www.nasmhpd.org*

Prescott, L. 2002. Veterans of abuse and daughters of the dark: The politics of naming and risk of transformation in building partnerships for change. Keynote address, 2nd annual convention of the International Society of Psychiatric Mental Health Nurses in Miami, FL.

The President's New Freedom Commission on Mental Health. 2003. Achieving the Promise: Transforming Mental Health Care in America. Executive Summary. DHHS Pub. No. SMA-03-3831. Rockville, MD.

Prochaska, J.O., and C.C. DiClemente. 1983. "Stages and processes of self-change of smoking: toward an integrative model of change." *Journal of Consulting and Clinical Psychology* 51 (3): 390–395.

Ray, N.K., K.J. Myers, and M.E. Rappaport. 1996. "Patient perspectives on restraint and seclusion experiences: A survey of former patients of New York State psychiatric facilities." *Psychiatric Rehabilitation Journal* 20: 11–18.

Senge, Peter. 1999. "The Leader's New Work: Building Learning Organizations." *Sloan Management Review*, 32 (1): 7–23.

Wadeson, H., and W. Carpenter. 1976. "Impact of the seclusion room experience." *Journal of Nervous and Mental Diseases* 163L: 318–328.